KV-050-912

INSTITUTIONS IN GLOBAL DISTRIBUTIVE JUSTICE

Studies in Global Justice and Human Rights
Series Editor: Thom Brooks

Immigration Justice
Peter W. Higgins

Rwanda and the Moral Obligation of Humanitarian Intervention
Joshua J. Kassner

Health Inequalities and Global Injustice
Patti Tamara Lenard and
Christine Straehle

The Morality of Peacekeeping
Daniel H. Levine

Institutions in Global Distributive Justice
András Miklós

Human Rights from Community
Oche Onazi

Retheorising Statelessness
Kelly Staples

www.euppublishing.com/series/sgjhr

INSTITUTIONS IN GLOBAL DISTRIBUTIVE JUSTICE

András Miklós

EDINBURGH
University Press

For my parents

© András Miklós, 2013

Edinburgh University Press Ltd
22 George Square, Edinburgh EH8 9LF
www.euppublishing.com

Typeset in 11/13 Palatino Light by
Servis Filmsetting Ltd, Stockport, Cheshire, and
printed and bound in Great Britain by
CPI Group (UK) Ltd, Croydon CR0 4YY

A CIP record for this book is available from the British Library

ISBN 978 0 7486 4471 1 (hardback)
ISBN 978 0 7486 4472 8 (webready PDF)
ISBN 978 0 7486 7822 8 (epub)
ISBN 978 0 7486 7821 1 (Amazon ebook)

The right of András Miklós to be identified as author of this work has
been asserted in accordance with the Copyright, Designs and Patents
Act 1988.

CONTENTS

ANALYTICAL TABLE OF CONTENTS

ACKNOWLEDGEMENTS

This book evolved from parts of my doctoral dissertation at Central European University. It went through countless iterations in writing and in classrooms where I taught some chapters as course materials. My work on this book was helped by several people and several organisations.

In the first place, I would like to thank János Kis who led me to thinking about global justice and who provided constant inspiration and patient support for my work during my graduate studies. It would be impossible to note all the points where I benefited from the ideas, comments and critical remarks with which he supplied me generously. My special thanks go to my friend Attila Tanyi who read the entire typescript in its penultimate version and provided me with valuable comments, criticisms and questions on many points.

I am also grateful to many others who provided feedback on earlier versions of various chapters. Among those I would like to thank are Norm Daniels, Thomas Pogge, Hugh LaFollette, Greg Bognár, Andrew Williams, Zoltán Miklósi, Alexander Astrov, Lars Vinx, Frank Adloff, Christine Chwaszcza, Robert Huseby, Cornelius Cappelen, Dag Einar Thorsen and audiences at various conferences. My students at the European University Institute and at the University of Rochester patiently endured their role as guinea pigs for many more or less successful arguments. Reflecting on their stimulating discussions in the classroom helped me improve many of these.

Financial support from several organisations allowed me to work on this book. I would like to thank the Central European University for providing me with a stimulating academic environment and supporting me financially during my graduate studies. I also thank the Foreign and Commonwealth Office (UK) for a Chevening Fellowship at Merton College, University of Oxford; the Research Council of Norway for a generous fellowship I held at the Ethics Programme and the Department of Philosophy, University of Oslo; the European University Institute for its Max Weber post-doctoral fellowship; and the Harvard University Program in Ethics and Health for a post-doctoral fellowship.

Above all, I would like to thank my wife, Jeanine, for her love and support without which the book would not have been possible.

Chapter 1

INTRODUCTION

Global justice is a relatively new topic in the history of political philosophy. A little over a decade ago, when I started working on problems of
global justice, there were very few books available in this field, written
by only a handful of theorists who were interested in this then marginal
topic.[1] Most works written on justice in political philosophy focused
on domestic issues, namely how the state should treat its citizens.
Recently, however, there has been an explosion of interest in questions
related to global justice, with an increase in the number of scholarly
works to match. This attention is fully justified, given the extreme level
of global poverty and the vast inequalities between peoples living in
the most affluent and in the poorest countries. We must ask what
the responsibilities of wealthier societies are. Do they have any duty
of justice to contribute to eradicating global poverty and reducing
inequalities? If they do, what are its grounds? Can we apply globally
the principles of justice we accept for the domestic domain? I seek to
approach and answer these questions by discussing whether there are
obligations of distributive justice that apply at the global level.

I should emphasise that this book is about global *distributive* justice,
and it refers only occasionally to other international areas to which the
concept of justice can be applied. Even though the concept of justice
is used in a large and growing literature as well as in public discourse
to evaluate a broad range of subjects both domestically and in the
global domain, including justifications of warfare and standards for the
conduct of war as well as civil and political liberties individuals are entitled to, my concern in this book is narrower. I am interested in what we
can say about justice as it concerns the distribution of socio-economic
goods at the global level. In particular, distributive justice concerns particularly stringent claims people have over relative or absolute shares of

things that are generally regarded valuable, such as the distribution of rights to income and wealth. The stringency of claims under justice can also be expressed by saying that people are entitled to their distributive shares, rather than being mere recipients of duties of beneficence, charity or humanity.

The book remains within the framework of liberal egalitarianism in distributive justice. It assumes that egalitarian requirements of distributive justice are part of an attractive position about domestic justice. It interprets egalitarianism in a broad sense: for our purposes egalitarianism requires the reduction of socio-economic inequalities. It need not require a complete equality of outcomes, however. For instance, the requirement to give priority to benefiting the worst-off members of society counts as an egalitarian requirement in this sense, even though it is compatible with sizeable social inequalities. Nor do I assume in this book that egalitarian policies should be pursued for the sake of equality as a value in itself. They might be justified by other considerations.

1.1 SOME BACKGROUND FACTS

There are well over two billion people in this world who live below $2 per day.[2] Some 1.29 billion people – close to one-fifth of the world's population – subsisted below the World Bank's official $1.25-a-day poverty line in 2008, which is considered the 'income or expenditure level below which a minimum, nutritionally adequate diet plus essential non-food requirements are not affordable' (Ravallion 2012; Pogge 2001a: 7). This poverty has dire consequences. Worldwide, the number of chronically undernourished people is around 800 million (UNDP 2004). Poverty-related causes, such as hunger and preventable diseases, result in around eighteen million deaths a year, accounting for roughly one-third of all human deaths (WHO 2004). More than ten million children, or 19 per cent of all human beings born into our world, die each year due to poverty-related causes (UNICEF 2005).

Beyond absolute levels of deprivation, the extent of global inequalities among the least-developed and wealthier countries is also striking. The poorest 44 per cent of the world's population consume only 1.3 per cent of the global output whereas the high-income countries, accounting for 15 per cent of the global population, consume about 81 per cent of it – a ratio of 62 to 1 (Pogge 2005b: 57).[3] Socio-economic inequalities have a profound impact on the lives of the poor. Life expectancy in Zimbabwe or Swaziland is about half that in Japan. Women giving birth in sub-Saharan Africa have about a seventy times higher chance to die in labour than their counterparts in a developed country (WHO 2007). The most striking inequality concerns the prospects faced by children under the age of five in the poorest and the wealthiest countries. If born in one of the least-developed countries, one is much more likely to die before reaching the age of five than someone born in one of the developed countries. For example, a child born in Mali has a sixty times higher chance of dying before the age of five than a child born in Norway (World Bank 2011). Moreover, according to some estimates, global trends also indicate a growth of inequality among wealthier and poorer parts of the world. These estimates show that the income gap between the poorest 20 per cent and the richest 20 per cent of the population rose from 1 to 30 in 1960 to 1 to 74 in 1997 (Pogge 2002: 100).[4]

1.2 UNIVERSAL MORAL DUTIES AND PARTICULARISTIC DISTRIBUTIVE REQUIREMENTS

When confronted with these extreme levels of poverty and inequality, we are compelled to think that better-off people have some obligations to help people who are much worse off, whether or not they are citizens of the same country. We recognise certain responsibilities that we have towards each of our fellow human beings. It is rarely contested that we have to avoid causing wrongful harm to others or that we should provide limited forms of assistance in certain contexts. For example, in the face of early deaths due to starvation or easily preventable diseases, it is arguable that inhabitants of affluent countries have a duty to provide humanitarian assistance to the desperately poor, especially when the costs of doing so are not too high. These responsibilities to our fellow humans are explained by the ideas, which seem natural for most people living in liberal democracies, that all human lives are of equal worth, or that all humans have certain basic rights.

Do we have obligations of justice to the global poor, though? Are dramatic global inequalities in life prospects also unjust, in addition to giving us humanitarian reasons to reduce suffering and prevent easily preventable deaths? There is a powerful intuition that supports an affirmative answer. Surely, the life of a newborn in Mali is no less valuable than the life of a newborn in Norway. It seems grossly unfair that the sheer accident of having been born in one country rather than in another can make such a huge difference to what one can expect in life. If we can do something to reduce these inequalities in life prospects, justice requires that we should do so. It seems that the assumption that the well-being of everybody matters equally will ultimately require that principles of justice have uninhibited global application.

On the other hand, many of us also think that we have particular duties to people with whom we stand in significant special relationships. We may have special responsibilities to friends or to members of our family which we think we do not owe to people in general. Similarly, many people take it for granted that the boundaries of their national political community carry moral weight, and that we have particular duties to our fellow citizens which we do not have to others.

There is a tension between according equal moral worth to all humans and acknowledging special responsibilities to our compatriots. One unwelcome result of this tension is that not only does the nation-state remain the basic unit of world politics but it is also all too often an unquestioned assumption in many theories of justice. Until very recently, much of political philosophy assumed that requirements of distributive justice hold among fellow citizens only but there are no such requirements at the global level. States were seen as the domain of distributive justice.

1.3 THE FOCUS ON INSTITUTIONS

To tackle this tension between the universalistic and particularistic strains within moral thought, I examine in this book whether special relationships matter for justice. In particular, I focus on the role that common institutions play in our thinking about justice. I will show that different understandings of the normative significance of institutions drive much of the current disagreement about whether or not requirements of justice have a global scope. Although the term 'institution' in a narrower sense can refer to organisations and collective bodies, my usage is broader than this. I follow John Rawls in regarding an institution as a public system of rules which defines positions together with their rights and duties (Rawls 1999a: 47–8, 55). Institutions thus understood include organisations – such as business firms or universities – but they also include systems of organisations – such as political systems and capitalist economies – and other institutions that do not involve organisations – such as simple barter economies

(S. Miller 2010). The institutions that are at the focus of this book have a number of further characteristics. First, they involve roles together with rights and duties attached to them. Second, I take an institution to be existing when a number of people regularly and knowingly follow its rules. Rather than considering institutions as abstract objects, that is, possible forms of conduct expressed by systems of rules, the book focuses on institutions as actual practices, that is, the way these rules are realised in the actions of persons. Viewed this way, institutions are constituted by the conduct of individuals upholding them. Third, many, though not all, institutions I am concerned with include formal sanctions to enforce their rules. The most important examples include legal and political systems, and economic institutions.

With this characterisation in mind, I analyse the roles that social, economic and political institutions play in conditioning the justification, the scope and the content of principles of justice. More specifically, I describe two different normative functions institutions have in theories of justice. First, I critically evaluate a number of positions about the role of institutions in generating requirements of distributive justice, and consider their implications for the scope of justice. Second, I develop a theory about the role political and economic institutions play in determining the content of requirements of distributive justice, and show how they can affect the scope of application of these requirements.

A number of distinctions will be important for the argument in this book. In particular, I will discuss three different aspects of theories of justice. The first aspect concerns the *scope* of justice, that is, the question 'what is the range of persons who have responsibilities to each other arising from considerations of justice?'[5] There are two contrasting positions to distinguish: cosmopolitanism and statism.[6] Cosmopolitans hold that the scope of distributive justice is global.[7] There are principles of distributive justice that include every human being within their scope. By contrast, statists argue that the scope of distributive justice is limited to a narrower range of persons such as citizens of the same state.[8] They deny that we have obligations of justice to foreigners though they allow for other sorts of obligation to them. Statists typically maintain that citizens of developed countries have several important but limited moral obligations to foreigners: they are required to respect the basic human rights of people in less-developed countries, to avoid causing undue harm to them, to provide humanitarian assistance to alleviate poverty and suffering, and to rescue the poorest from hunger-related death.

Contrary to what cosmopolitans claim, however, citizens of affluent countries do not have obligations of distributive justice to people in other countries. It is useful to distinguish further two cosmopolitan positions according to how they view domestic requirements of justice in comparison with global requirements. One cosmopolitan position – what Simon Caney calls 'ambitious cosmopolitanism' – holds that the requirements of justice we owe to our compatriots are the same as the requirements we owe to foreigners (Caney 2005: 105). The second – moderate – cosmopolitan position grants that we have obligations of justice to compatriots and to foreigners but maintains that the former demand considerably more than the latter. The book thus distinguishes three positions with regard to the question 'how do our distributive obligations to compatriots compare to our obligations to foreigners?', two of which are cosmopolitan, one statist.

The second distinction concerns what we might call the *ground* of justice, describing morally relevant features necessary to give rise to requirements of justice. In particular, I will distinguish between two contrasting views about the role special relations play in generating requirements of justice. Relational conceptions of justice hold that individuals' standing in a specific practice-mediated relation is a necessary condition for requirements of distributive justice to exist among them.[9] The relevant practices are forms of public rule-governed behaviour, with typical examples of a special relation being institutions that regulate social and economic relations among persons.[10] Think about the legal system and other economic and social institutions that circumscribe property and structure the economy. These institutions have been regarded as necessary for the existence of justice relation for a number of reasons: because they have a profound and pervasive effect on the lives of their subjects; because they employ coercive force against their subjects; or because they authoritatively govern cooperative schemes among their participants.[11] Relational theories regard these relations as playing a *foundational* role in grounding requirements of justice. By contrast, non-relational views deny this and claim that at least some demands of justice can emerge even in the absence of practice-mediated relations. Political or economic institutions do not ground all requirements of justice.

It is useful to approach the problem of the scope of justice by discussing the ground of justice because the two are related. In the current literature, much of the disagreement between cosmopolitans and statists about the scope of justice has been motivated by different views about the role political and economic institutions play in grounding justice. In particular, statist views are grounded in relational conceptions of justice whereas cosmopolitanism has been defended on both non-relational and relational grounds. Disagreement about the ground of justice can lead to disagreement about the scope of justice in two ways. First, non-relational theories of justice are cosmopolitan. They allow for demands of justice to exist among humans even in the absence of practice-mediated relationships. The scope of justice in a relational view, however, will be contingent on the kinds of relation we stand in with others. Absent the requisite relation at the global level, there will be no global requirements of justice. So we might disagree about the scope of justice depending on whether we are relationists or non-relationists. Second, if we are relationists, we might be cosmopolitans or statists depending on *what kind* of relation we regard as foundational for grounding justice.

The third distinction concerns how institutions relate to the *content* of justice. According to the standard view, institutions are effective instruments to carry out requirements of justice that apply independently from these institutions. The content of these requirements is given independently from, and prior to, the rules of institutions. What institutions do is overcome some of the shortcomings moral agents have and help them more effectively to discharge their justice-based obligations. A different view of institutions regards them as playing a constitutive role in determining the content of justice. Fundamental principles of justice do not fully specify just distributive shares or what we ought to do with regard to justice. Existing economic and political institutions partially constitute the content of justice by specifying these.

1.4 AN OVERVIEW OF THE BOOK

The book consists of two main parts. First, Chapters 2 to 6 evaluate arguments regarding the scope of justice by analysing assumptions about the role of institutions in grounding justice. Second, Chapter 7 advances a position about the role institutions play in determining the content of justice. With regard to the scope of justice, the book defends a cosmopolitan conception of distributive justice in which the scope of justice is not limited to nation-states. I argue against statist positions that limit the scope of distributive justice to national political communities on the basis of various relational conceptions of justice. Chapters 2 to 5 critically discuss different relational theories of justice that regard national ties or domestic institutions and policies regulating social and economic inequalities as necessary to generate requirements of distributive justice. These institutions and policies are regarded as foundational insofar as they employ coercive force against their subjects, or authoritatively regulate cooperation among fellow citizens, or have a profound and pervasive effect on individual lives. My argument demonstrates that these relational theories cannot justify statism. Their most plausible version will yield a relational cosmopolitan conclusion. Chapter 6 rehearses non-relational arguments that could justify some requirements of distributive justice outside institutionally governed interaction. They defend the position that distributive requirements can exist on different grounds, such as by virtue of our common humanity or competing claims by agents to scarce natural resources. Global institutions may not be necessary to generate global requirements of justice.

Having discussed the role of institutions in generating requirements of distributive justice, the book provides a detailed account of a distinct normative function institutions perform by determining the content of principles of justice. Chapter 7 argues that political and economic institutions can limit the applicability of principles of justice even in a cosmopolitan conception. It shows that, in the absence of existing institutions, fundamental principles of justice are not determinate enough for assessing alternative distributive shares and for guiding and evaluating individual conduct and institutional design. Therefore, they cannot be applied with a global scope to adjudicate all distributive issues even in non-relational cosmopolitan egalitarian theories. Political and economic institutions partially constitute the content of justice and enable the application of principles of justice by determining fair distributive shares and by resolving indeterminacies about justice-based requirements resulting from strategic interaction and disagreement. Institutions can affect the application of principles of justice even when they do not give rise to them. This view of institutions does not amount to a relational conception of justice, however. It is compatible with holding that some requirements of justice can exist independently from, and prior to, coercive political institutions.

Working within the framework of liberal egalitarianism, the findings of the book are twofold. First, even though the book is not meant as a fully fledged defence of egalitarianism, it does present an intuitive case for it and argues that, if there are reasons to accept distributive egalitarianism in the domestic case, then there are equally compelling reasons to accept it for the global domain. Second, the book breaks new ground by providing a detailed analysis of how political and economic institutions specify the content of requirements of distributive justice, and shows that existing institutions can limit the scope of application of these requirements even in a non-relational cosmopolitan theory.

Notes

1 Philosophers who set the scene included Peter Singer, Onora O'Neill, Thomas Nagel, Charles Beitz, Thomas Pogge, and Henry Shue, among others (Singer, 1972; O'Neill, 1974; Nagel, 1977; Beitz, 1999; Pogge, 1989; Shue, 1996).
2 The figure was 2.47 billion in 2008 (Ravallion, 2012).
3 The figures are adjusted so as to reflect purchasing power in the domestic product. If compared at market rates, the differences would be even greater, amounting to a ratio of 180 between high-income and low-income countries.
4 Pogge based his claim on the 1999 UNDP development report. Others question this claim, however (Singer, 2002, pp. 81–2; Risse, 2005a, p. 10).
5 See Abizadeh, 2007, p. 323 for this characterisation of the problem of the scope of justice.
6 Cosmopolitanism and statism are not logical opposites. We can think of non-cosmopolitan theories that do not limit the scope of justice to citizens of the same state. The scope of justice can be limited by other conditions. Contrasting cosmopolitanism with statism is justified, however, because all non-cosmopolitan theories that have been recently defended are statist.
7 When describing cosmopolitanism, I should make it clear that I shall be concerned with cosmopolitanism about *justice*, in accordance with the usage of the term in contemporary literature. Even though the term 'cosmopolitanism' has a long history, I do not discuss pre-modern conceptions of cosmopolitanism. The term originally goes back to ancient Greek times. In the form of *kosmopolitēs* – 'citizen of the universe' – it was first used by Cynics and Stoics, referring to an ethical stance that does not regard one's political membership as having any foundational relevance for one's identities, loyalties, and responsibilities. Contemporary cosmopolitans find the moral underpinnings of some of these versions of cosmopolitanism unpalatable. For instance, in its Stoic use, cosmopolitanism was viewed as part of an ethical doctrine that regarded all humans as citizens of a

perfect rational order, who live in agreement with the law governing the cosmos (Brown and Kleingeld, 2002). Contemporary cosmopolitans focus instead on what standards institutions should meet, what policies should be pursued by governments, and what actions individuals are required to take to meet requirements of justice in the face of certain facts about the world as it exists today.

 8 Some recent examples of the statist position include (Miller, 2007; Sangiovanni, 2007; Sangiovanni, 2008; Nagel, 2005; Blake, 2001); some prominent recent articles from the cosmopolitan side include (Abizadeh, 2007; Cohen and Sabel, 2006; Julius, 2006).

 9 I borrow the term 'relational conception of justice' from Andrea Sangiovanni who defines relational conceptions of distributive justice as holding that the 'practice-mediated relations in which individuals stand condition the content, scope, and justification of those principles' (Sangiovanni, 2007, p. 5). As he himself acknowledges, however, 'the distinction between relational and non-relational conception is a distinction about the grounds of justice' (Sangiovanni, 2007, p. 8); therefore, I shall take relational conceptions of justice to be making a claim about the role of certain relations in grounding demands of justice. We shall see later that such conceptions do not immediately settle questions about the scope of principles nor do they immediately determine the content of justice. I regard Sangiovanni as a representative of the relational view because he holds that 'principles of distributive justice cannot be formulated or justified independently of the practices they are intended to regulate' (Sangiovanni, 2007, p. 5).

10 I use the word 'practice' in Rawls's sense, referring to 'any form of activity specified by a system of rules which defines offices, roles, moves, penalties, defences, and so on, and which gives the activity its structure' (Rawls, 1999c, p. 20). Institutions can be regarded as a special case of practices.

11 See the discussion by Abizadeh (2007).

Chapter 2

NATIONALIST THEORIES OF JUSTICE

I started this book by asking questions about the scope of justice. Are there any requirements of distributive justice applying globally? If so, are these the same requirements as those that apply domestically, or different? I will approach these questions about the scope of justice first by discussing the ground of justice, evaluating positions about morally relevant features necessary to give rise to requirements of justice. This chapter critically evaluates a family of positions that highlight the normative significance of the special relationship between fellow nationals.[1] They hold that relatively demanding requirements of socio-economic justice apply only among fellow nationals by virtue of the special relationship they stand in with one another. Nationalists make two different kinds of claim. Some nationalists argue that there are no distributive requirements that apply outside national communities. Others claim that, even if there might be international distributive requirements, these are significantly weaker and different in kind than requirements of distributive justice that apply only among fellow nationals. This position can be summed up in the thesis that fellow nationals take priority.[2] What is common to both claims is that they regard international distributive requirements as substantially different from what we owe to our fellow nationals. Nationalists draw a stark contrast between principles of justice regulating the national domain and principles for regulating international affairs, and claim that the former demand substantially more from us than the latter.

To understand nationalism better we have to describe briefly what a nation is. There are at least three different versions of nationalism depending on how one characterises nations. Civic nationalism regards nations as comprised of citizens of the same state. Ethnic nationalists hold that nations are made up of people sharing a common ethnic

identity. Although both civic and ethnic nationalism have their advocates, the most influential versions of nationalism regard nations as
cultural communities (Miller 1995; Tamir 1995). According to cultural
conceptions of nationalism, a nation consists of people sharing a
common culture. What elements of a culture are relevant for nationality
is controversial. Nationalists cite common language, common history,
shared connection to a territory, shared beliefs and mutual commit-
ment as examples, among other features. Unless otherwise indicated, I
will consider nations as cultural communities without further specifying which elements of culture define nations.

I distinguish between three kinds of arguments that have been
offered by nationalists for special domestic distributive requirements.
One argument rests on a relativistic view of justice, whereas the other
two emphasise special benefits generated by national political communities. The chapter is organised as follows. I first consider and reject
an argument against international distributive requirements relying
on Michael Walzer's view about the social meanings of goods. The
second part of the chapter considers non-relativistic arguments against
demanding global distributive requirements. It distinguishes between
arguments emphasising the instrumental and non-instrumental value
of national attachments respectively, and argues that neither version
can justify the nationalist thesis. Before I present the arguments,
however, I briefly sketch the moral universalist outlook that cosmopolitans rely on.

2.1 INDIVIDUALIST MORAL UNIVERSALISM AND
COSMOPOLITAN JUSTICE

Cosmopolitanism, as well as some non-cosmopolitan theories, are
based on the premise that all humans are of equal worth and their lives
and well-being are equally important from the moral point of view. This
general outlook is thought by cosmopolitans to justify certain requirements on the design of institutions, on the actions of individuals, and
on the distribution of resources. Because I describe cosmopolitanism
in the Introduction and in Chapter 6, I do not discuss here the content
of these requirements. Let me briefly mention, however, some of the
characteristics of the underlying general moral stance as a backdrop to
the argument against nationalism.

The ground for the cosmopolitan outlook is a general individualist moral universalism which has the following defining features.[3] It is individualistic, holding that only individual human beings have ultimate moral value: the moral value of other things, such as institutions, political communities, culture, relationships and so on, is always derivative. It is universal, in the sense that it regards every human being as having ultimate moral value; thus, it forbids attaching no moral value at all to some human beings. Furthermore, it accords equal concern to all humans, recognising that each of us has equal moral value, which rules out weighting the value of individuals differently in our moral thinking on the basis of features such as race, sex, or ethnicity. Finally, the scope of validity of this outlook is general, holding that individuals are of ultimate moral value for everyone: there are fundamental moral values that are valid across the world, binding everyone.

On the basis of this general moral stance, cosmopolitans hold the thesis that there are international requirements of distributive justice. Furthermore, more ambitious forms of cosmopolitanism maintain that international distributive principles roughly resemble the domestic principles of justice we are familiar with from liberal theories of justice.

Nationalists challenge the cosmopolitan conclusion. Their arguments sometimes proceed by attacking one or several of the main features of this moral stance, that is, individualism, universality, equal concern and generality. The next section considers one such argument. It is important to note, however, that not all nationalists pursue this strategy: as we shall see later there are attempts to justify the nationalist thesis which are compatible with individualistic moral universalism.

2.2 RELATIVISM ABOUT JUSTICE

2.2.1 *The argument from the social meanings of goods*

The first nationalist argument has been put forward by communitarian theorists who see the scope of principles of justice as limited on the basis of a relativistic view of morality.[4] Whereas moral universalism holds that there are some moral values or demands that are valid across the world, moral relativism denies that fundamental moral standards are universal and affirms that different agents are subject to different basic moral requirements, depending on prevailing social customs, practices, beliefs and conventions (Harman 1989: 371). For each society, the correct moral principles are those that conform to the society's commonly affirmed standards.

We can distinguish two versions of the relativist claim. The extreme view holds that all moral values are relative to societies. The more moderate view allows for some universal values but maintains that there are some moral values that are relative (Caney 2005: 30). I shall discuss Michael Walzer's moderate-version relativism, as he is specifically concerned with distributive justice. Walzer's theory does not rule out some universal moral demands but maintains that, in the domain of distributive justice, values are relative to societies. The Walzerian theory rules out globally valid requirements of justice because it holds that the application of principles of justice requires a shared social understanding both about distributive principles and about the meaning of goods, and it assumes that no such understanding exists globally. Walzer argues that principles of justice guiding the distribution of goods in societies are not intelligible in abstraction from existing political communities (Walzer 1983: 28–30). Principles of justice valid for a given political community are defined by the shared understandings of the members of the community. A given set of principles of justice applies to a political community where members' shared understandings imply this set. What motivates this position is Walzer's belief that 'all distributions are just or unjust relative to the social meanings of the goods at stake', and these social meanings, as well as the distributive principles they imply, are relative to particular cultures (Walzer 1983: 9). There are no global requirements of distributive justice because no comparable interpretive community exists globally.

The argument is worth spelling out in more detail. First, distributive justice in Walzer's view is concerned with the distribution of social goods: *all* goods whose distribution is a concern of justice are social goods such as education, health care or food (Walzer 1983: 7). Furthermore, the meaning as well as the value of goods that justice is in the business of distributing are specific to societies. For instance, education in the medieval Jewish communities meant something different from what education means in contemporary America: it prepared adult men for '[participation] in religious services and in discussions of religious doctrine' (Walzer 1983: 76). This good was of no concern for women who played no such role in religious practice. Likewise, disability provision had a different meaning in ancient Athens because disability itself was understood in different terms from our contemporary understanding.

Assuming these goods have no natural meanings, Walzer holds that their meanings are defined by the shared understandings of societies through a social process of interpretation (Walzer 1983: 7–8). Walzer also assumes that the meaning of a good and its distributive criterion are intertwined: there are no criteria for distributing social goods that are independent from the very meanings of the goods as they are understood in a society (Walzer 1983: 9). The distribution of education or disability provisions is guided by communities' understanding of the meaning and the point of these goods: because the point of education in medieval Jewish communities made no reference to women, they were not included in its distribution. Walzer thus argues that distributive criteria are inherently social as well. He regards nation-states as the exclusive domain for distributive justice because he assumes that cultures, by reference to which goods and distributive principles attached to them are defined, are unique to political communities.

The political and social institutions of nation-states occupy an important role in Walzer's theory. Institutions have historically shaped the character of nations as distributive communities and thus current cultural beliefs about goods and about how they should be distributed within society. Furthermore, contingent existing institutions provide the framework for social dialogue within which interpretation takes place. If so, the institutions of nation-states ground requirements of distributive justice because specific requirements exist only by virtue of shared institutions that shape the interpretive processes of national communities.

Could Walzer's theory allow for principles of justice with a global scope? There are currently no worldwide criteria to guide distribution in the global domain, because Walzer argues that the meanings of goods differ across societies (Walzer 1983: 8). Could we come up with a list of abstract goods that are general enough to be applicable globally for the purpose of defining a just global distribution even though, at present, goods with which justice is concerned and the principles of justice that should guide their distribution vary across cultures? If we could come up with such a list, there could be a shared global understanding of principles of global justice which would govern the distribution of basic goods globally. Global principles in turn would be translated into distributive arrangements concerning more specific goods by individual societies in accordance with their shared understandings of these goods. Walzer denies this possibility, however: he believes it is impossible to construct a list of goods that, on the one hand make the same sense in all cultures, and, on the other, are concrete enough to be able to serve as a standard for distribution (Walzer 1983: 8). To recall, he thinks distributive principles are always relative to concrete goods with specific meanings, and the further abstract goods are removed from these concrete ones, the less determinate the standards guiding their distribution will be. Justice is about social goods that make up their own 'distributive spheres' in which distribution is determined by their own specific criteria.

Walzer's theory of justice can be criticised from a number of directions. For instance, it can be criticised in its general form as a version of cultural relativism about moral principles. Relativism has been criticised for, among other things: sanctioning morally abhorrent conduct if it is in line with existing cultural practices; for being self-defeating in the case of cultures that subscribe to universal values; for being inconsistent if relativism is affirmed as a universal truth; and for not being able to make sense of genuine disagreement. I do not discuss these general criticisms of moral relativism and will rather focus on criticising Walzer's specific version of it because it may have greater initial plausibility, given its focus on differences between distributive principles affirmed by various societies. Walzer's theory has a more limited scope than the theories presented by other relativists that confine the validity of all moral principles to cultural communities with shared understandings. It focuses on distributive justice, a field that is much more controversial than some other areas of morality, such as basic human rights. This might be thought to create a prima facie case for Walzer's distributive pluralism. A strategy defending Walzer's relativism about justice might then proceed by drawing a distinction between basic moral norms about which there is a prospect for international agreement, and requirements of distributive justice that are inescapably limited to domestic societies.

Let us see if this more limited Walzerian thesis is defensible. I will now examine two aspects of the thesis that might rule out considerations of global justice. As we saw, for the application of considerations of justice, Walzer requires a social consensus both about distributive principles and about the meaning and value of goods that need to be distributed, and assumes that consensus exists only in the domestic context. I will first argue against the empirical claim that there is much more radical disagreement about distributive requirements internationally than domestically. Next, I will show that requiring shared understandings about the meaning and value of goods in a theory of justice cannot be justified.

2.2.2 The contrast between global disagreement and domestic consensus

One reason why Walzerian theory rules out the existence of global distributive requirements is that it requires a shared social understanding about distributive principles and assumes that no such understanding exists globally. Talk about global justice is unintelligible because there is a sharp contrast between the domestic and global domains: there is domestic consensus about principles governing the distribution of various goods but there is no such consensus internationally. Because the application of justice presupposes a shared social understanding about its requirements, principles of justice apply only where social consensus about these exists, that is, in the domestic context. The first argument against Walzer, offered by Allen Buchanan, questions the degree and intractability of global distributive disagreement on which Walzer builds his sceptical thesis about principles of global justice. This is an empirical argument: it aims to show that the supposed contrast between a largely homogeneous public opinion about matters of domestic distributive justice and irresolvable international disagreement about matters of global justice is false, and that there is greater international consensus than relativists acknowledge (Buchanan 2004: 204–5).

Political communities are not homogeneous in the moral values of their members: in pluralistic societies, members deeply disagree about moral issues, and disagreement is especially intractable with regard to issues of distributive justice. This makes the assumption about the existence of a contrast between domestic and international societies ungrounded. If Walzer's theory presupposes complete consensus about distributive matters, it is difficult to see how considerations of justice could be applied even in the domestic context. If less than complete consensus is required, arguably the beginnings of such a global consensus are present. Furthermore, there seems to be little reason to believe that domestic disagreement is more likely to be resolved in the long run than the international one. A claim that this is so should be supported by empirical evidence which neither Walzer nor other communitarians provide (Buchanan 2004: 204). We are still in an early phase of international interdependence and cultural interaction, and it seems premature to conclude, on the basis of a somewhat greater level of international disagreement about distributive justice, that – in contrast with domestic disagreement – international disputes are less likely to reach consensus in the long run. Consider the evolution and growing acceptance of international standards of human rights: at the beginning of the twentieth century it would have seemed entirely unrealistic to expect states to give up significant portions of their sovereignty by subscribing to international norms of human rights which they nevertheless did in the course of the second half of the century.

A further point undermining the claim concerning the pervasiveness of international disagreement about distributive principles is that considerations of fairness and distributive justice actually already figure in, and increasingly pervade, international law, the practices of supranational organisations, and discussions about them. Considerations of justice have been institutionalised by a growing number of international norms and in the practices of supranational institutions. This fact indicates that there is some convergence about issues of justice in the international domain (Franck 1995). Areas where considerations of distributive justice play a prominent role include the following:

1. the World Trade Organization's Technical Barriers to Trade allowing for human rights and labour standards to be used in restricting free trade;
2. the International Labor Organization's requirement for member states to end discrimination and child labour, and to promote freedom of expression and collective bargaining;
3. subsidised loans by multilateral lending institutions to support economic growth and reduce poverty in poorer countries;
4. obligations imposed by multilateral environmental agreements on states to take into account the interests of citizens of other countries and future generations by the conservation of a fair share of natural resources;
5. multilateral treaties governing the exploitation of natural resources on the seabed and continental shelves and the distribution of benefits from their use;
6. treaties regulating the use of outer space and Antarctica, regarding them as the 'common heritage' of humankind (Cohen and Sabel 2006; Franck 1995: 436; Buchanan 2004: 205–6).

These examples indicate that, in a number of well-circumscribed areas in international law and practices, there is a growing consensus not only about the importance of distributive justice but also about the judgement that certain distributive arrangements are clearly unjust. This makes a compelling case against scepticism about the possibility of reaching an international agreement on matters of distributive justice even if at present there is no consensus on everything that distributive justice is thought to require.

Of course, these considerations do not show that there is an international consensus about a full conception of distributive justice. But then nor is there such a consensus domestically. What examples of the international fairness discourse show is that it is a mistake to believe that considerations of distributive justice play no role at all in the international domain, and that current disagreements make it impossible to make progress towards a growing consensus. Because Walzer's empirical point does not hold and there is considerable global consensus about matters of justice, the normative conclusion denying the global application of considerations of justice does not follow. Even if the application of justice requires a degree of social consensus about requirements of justice, the global application of principles of justice is not defeated.

2.2.3 *The role of goods in distributive justice*

Besides disagreement about distributive principles, the second reason why there is no room for globally valid requirements of distributive justice in the Walzerian theory is that there are no shared understandings across cultures about the meaning and value of various goods. I shall now argue, however, that no such shared understanding is necessary for making distributive decisions. The second argument against Walzer's distributive pluralism targets his scepticism about the possibility of finding a set of abstract goods that, on the one hand, is general enough to be applicable globally and, on the other, is specific enough to support a standard of distribution. I will show, first, that abstract goods, such as primary goods or resources, are, indeed, capable of providing standards for an interpersonal valuation of goods that can be used for distribution. Second, I shall argue that a liberal theory of justice cannot accept the Walzerian premise that all goods that are subject to distribution under principles of justice should be distributed in accordance with their own inherent distributive criteria.

Abstract goods without a shared social meaning can be applied to measuring the value of distribuenda across cultures. Consider the way markets work. Markets operate on the assumption that, within the limits of a permissible range of goods, 'anything can be traded for anything'. This idea is institutionalised in the use of money as a medium of exchange, making it possible for any pair of traders to exchange goods even without having a clear idea about what goods they want to hold eventually (Waldron 1995: 144). So, as a matter of general fact, markets do not distribute individual goods on the basis of specific criteria built into their meanings. Goods get distributed in markets on the basis of their worth to individual participants. Thus, as long as global markets exist, lack of agreement about the value of a good across cultures does not preclude global distribution. Goods can be traded among market actors even when they differ in their valuation of the good they want to exchange. The working of markets shows that it is possible to rely on some very abstract measure, such as money, in the interpersonal valuation of concrete goods that need to be distributed.[5]

Not only are abstract goods sufficient for the application of distributive justice, it is also desirable to determine the just distribution on the basis of such goods. Communities that distribute concrete goods in accordance with their inherent distributive criteria are arguably unjust. Consider Walzer's assumption that citizens in a nation-state agree on the meaning and value of goods as well as on the way they should be distributed because nations share a language, historical consciousness, and culture to a sufficiently large extent to ensure that they make up distinct distributive communities. In effect, Walzer presupposes that members of political communities agree in their conceptions of the good. In a liberal theory of justice, however, goods are not regarded as having their own distributive criteria built into their very meaning. On the contrary, people differ in their opinions about the value of certain goods because they have differing conceptions of the good, different ideas of what gives value to life, and different preferences. Some would have more beauty products while others would rather choose to go on a hiking trip; some drink champagne while others prefer beer; some would want to go more often to opera while others would rather watch more television. In each of these pairs of goods some people would be willing to spend more of their resources on some goods rather than on others. If society decided to allocate concrete goods equally on the basis of a specific understanding of their value, some individuals would find that they are unfairly disadvantaged as compared to others. To prevent unfairness, the goods that distributive justice is concerned with should be valued in a way that takes account of the differing conceptions of the good people have, and takes account of them equally. Equal concern for the well-being of everyone affected requires that we measure well-being for purposes of distributive justice in a way that is neutral across various conceptions of the good individuals hold.[6] This is why John Rawls in his theory of justice proposes a list of 'primary goods' as the metric of just distribution, rather than holding that goods ought to be distributed in a way that reflects their inherent distributive criteria as they are understood in a given society (Rawls 1999a). Actual or hypothetical markets may also provide a standard for the interpersonal comparison of resource levels that is not biased towards any conception of the good life. Considerations like this motivate Ronald Dworkin to take resources as the metric of distribution in his egalitarian theory of justice (Dworkin 2000).[7] Walzer's theory about the social meaning of goods and their distributive criteria is biased towards some conceptions of the good, hence it does not pay equal respect to the interests of all individuals among whom the problem of distribution arises.

To conclude, Walzer's requirement that goods are to be distributed in accordance with their social meanings is neither necessary for the application of justice, nor is it desirable if justice is to avoid favouring the preferences of some people at the expense of others. Justice requires that we measure individual well-being in terms of abstract goods, such as primary goods or resources, which provide an unbiased standard of interpersonal comparison. These abstract goods do not have inherent distributive criteria built into their meaning: their distribution should be guided by distributive principles we arrive at independently of the meanings of goods to specific communities.

2.3 PRIORITY TO FELLOW NATIONALS

Let us consider a second group of arguments against the cosmopolitan position which is not related to relativism about justice. In the remaining part of this chapter I discuss the view that involvement in special relationships that national communities represent brings with it special distributive requirements. The main thesis of theoretical nationalism, a prominent doctrine advanced in various forms by contemporary authors, is that people are permitted or required to be partial to their own nations and fellow nationals because they stand in a special relationship with them. In other words, nationalists hold that we owe more to our fellow nationals than we do to other people in distributive matters. What forms of partiality nationalists have in mind and what degree of it they regard as acceptable are rarely specified and remain controversial.[8] Whatever the exact form and degree nationalists think national partiality should take, they regard distributive requirements among fellow nationals as substantially more demanding than distributive requirements to outsiders. We are required by justice to give priority to the interests and needs of our fellow nationals over the interests and needs of people elsewhere in the world. Earlier I distinguished two versions of the nationalist position. The stronger claim stated that there are no distributive obligations to outsiders, whereas the weaker claim allowed for distributive obligations to fellow nationals and to outsiders, but it held that the former demand significantly more than the latter. I shall evaluate two different strategies to justify one or the other of these claims: an instrumental justification of national partiality and non-instrumental considerations of the value of national self-determination.

2.3.1 Instrumental justification

The instrumental justification emphasises the value of national partiality for impartial justice. It starts from impartial fundamental moral principles that consider the interests of all humans equally and shows that partiality for fellow nationals is justified because it has good effects impartially considered. One version of this strategy is represented by what Robert Goodin calls the assigned responsibility model. Following a consequentialist reasoning, Goodin argues that fellow nationals are better placed to look after the interests of one another and are therefore required to give priority to one another's interests on universalistic grounds (Goodin 1988).[9] Goodin's strategy views special relations among fellow nationals as a useful convention where particularistic duties are 'an administrative device for discharging our general duties more efficiently' (Goodin 1988: 685). Morality in many cases requires that specific agents are assigned specific responsibilities in the interest of all. Consider the analogy of a lifeguard on the beach: a person is singled out to fulfil a general duty to rescue others in distress because appointing one person as a lifeguard can overcome coordination problems that might be created by many more people rushing to the rescue of a drowning person than necessary. As a consequence, ordinary beachgoers are relieved of their duty to rescue others from the water (Goodin 1988: 680–1). By analogy, fellow nationals are relieved of their duties of justice towards members of other nations because these nations are assigned responsibility for the interests of their own members. This justification of national partiality is instrumental because it proceeds by showing that a set of distributive rules incorporating national partiality produces the best overall set of outcomes from a point of view that takes the interests of all humans equally into account.

One thing to note about this argument is that it leaves open the question of how to circumscribe the group of people who should be partial to one another. Earlier I distinguished several interpretations of nationalism, each of which provides a different answer to this question. Ethnic nationalists would advocate the position that people belonging to a common ethnic group ought to be partial to one another. Civic nationalists would hold that we owe more to our fellow citizens. Cultural nationalists would argue that people sharing a national culture have special obligations to one another. From the premise that specific agents should bear special responsibility for the welfare of others it does not obviously follow that people sharing a common culture have special obligations to one another; in other words, the argument does not vindicate cultural nationalism. To establish this conclusion, the further point must be shown that impartial moral principles are more efficiently discharged if they are broken down to special duties among people sharing a common national culture. In Chapter 4, I shall evaluate an argument to this effect by David Miller and John Rawls who argue that people motivated by a shared sense of nationality are more willing to make sacrifices for one another and, for this reason, principles of justice are more likely to be implemented successfully in nation-states. Let us set aside this point for now and see if the assigned responsibility model can justify partiality to fellow nationals, whichever way nationality is understood.

Instrumental justifications cannot show that, at the fundamental level, we owe more to our fellow nationals than we do to outsiders. They assume that the interests of all humans are to be treated equally and they argue that this is better done through particularlistic duties to fellow nationals. Particularistic duties, however, do not add anything to our existing obligations at the fundamental level: ultimately, what we owe to fellow nationals is the same as what we owe to human beings in general.

Can the instrumental argument justify national partiality at a less basic level of ethical requirements? Can we have distributive obligations to our fellow nationals that are substantially different from our obligations to outsiders? It is unlikely that the argument can even show this much, given some plausible assumptions about the impact of national partiality on the global distribution and about what considerations impartial moral evaluation should take into account (Beitz 1983: 593). Let me explain.

National partiality under the circumstances of existing global inequality is unlikely to produce the best overall result from an impartial perspective. The justification of special responsibilities would have to presuppose a more equal global distribution of resources against which nations' taking care of the interests of their members might be desirable (Goodin 1988: 685). Inequalities between the richest and poorest nations in the world are vast, however. Greater international redistribution could prevent so many easily preventable deaths and so much suffering at relatively little cost that it arguably produces a better state of affairs impartially considered. It is very unlikely that a set-up where the governments of Mali and Norway are each exclusively responsible for the well-being of their own citizens produces the best overall state of affairs from an impartial point of view. Furthermore, an arrangement where each nation would be allocated an equal initial per capita share of the Earth's resources, and then left free to do whatever it can to perform its special responsibility for its members, could still be unjust if nations are not self-sufficient. Unless one takes a libertarian position with a minimal conception of background justice, it seems plausible to argue that the operation of free markets tends to generate injustice unless it takes place against the background of just institutions correcting for unfavourable distributive effects. Consider the analogy of partiality to family members or friends in domestic societies: such partiality is generally regarded as permissible, if at all, only when there are background institutions in place that implement the impartial requirements of justice. Individuals have a duty to create and uphold such institutions that maintain the conditions of impartiality, against the background of which communal projects and personal commitments can take place. For instance, I ought not to evade paying my fair share of taxes just because a friend of mine is in need. Showing special concern for the interests of those near and dear to us can be permitted only once we have contributed our fair share to impartial institutions. Analogously, if just global institutions are in place that maintain a fair background distribution and correct for unjust distributive effects of market transactions, there may indeed be legitimate cases of giving priority to fellow nationals. Given plausible assumptions about background justice, however, instrumental arguments cannot show that distributive obligations to fellow nationals are substantially different from obligations to outsiders.

2.3.2 *Non-instrumental justifications*

I now turn to non-instrumental justifications of national partiality which pose a more significant challenge to cosmopolitanism. Such justifications do not defend national partiality by pointing out its instrumental role in bringing about a state of affairs that is desirable from a perspective considering the interests of all humans equally. Rather, they claim that the relationship between fellow nationals is in itself sufficient to warrant special distributive requirements that do not apply among humans as such.

Unlike ethical relativism, these arguments for the special distributive status of relational facts do not restrict the scope of validity of ethical reasoning. The nationalist doctrine can be non-relativistic. It can take at least one ethical principle as having universal validity, namely the principle that special relations are of intrinsic importance and carry with them special distributive requirements among participants. Members of every national community ought to be partial to their fellow members because this requirement applies universally and not only within those cultures whose norms include a requirement of such partiality. On the other hand, the doctrine is not instrumental because it prescribes partiality to one's own fellow nationals without justifying partiality by reference to its desirability from an impartial perspective.

We should distinguish two basic rationales for the nationalist claim. One position regards some goods provided by nationhood as good impersonally, and justifies special duties among fellow nationals by showing that they are necessary for securing these goods. The other strategy proceeds by showing that special relations between compatriots have a substantial effect on their lives. The importance of these relations comes from their effect on individual well-being and underwrites special distributive requirements. Let's see each of these arguments in turn.

2.3.3 *The impersonal value of national self-determination*

The first group of arguments holds that national partiality is justified partly because some goods provided by nationhood, such as the survival or flourishing of national culture, or national self-determination, are good impersonally and require special duties among fellow nationals. This strategy regards these goods as good impersonally in the sense that they are 'not reducible to the goods of individual persons, or to goods located in individual persons' lives' (Hurka 1997: 144). The reason why one should show greater concern for the survival or flourishing of one's national culture, or the self-determination of the nation one belongs to, is not that these values bear on the interests of one's fellow nationals but the importance of these things in themselves. Cultures and relationships figure in moral reasoning as foundational elements: their normative force does not derive from their effects on the well-being of individuals.

A number of impersonal goods have been associated with nationhood and thought to justify special distributive requirements. For instance, some communitarian authors – most straightforwardly, perhaps, Charles Taylor – argue that the cultural survival of national groups and national minorities, for example, the survival of French culture in Quebec, is good. It is a good not only in the sense of being good for the Quebecois as individual persons but also good in itself: it would be a good thing if francophone culture in Quebec survived even if this would not be better for anybody (Taylor 1994: 58; Hurka 1997: 145). The implications of the importance of cultural survival for international distributive justice are not clear, however. As long as we do not think that the impersonal value of national cultures justifies special distributive obligations to compatriots, we can grant that national cultures are good impersonally without accepting the nationalist point.

How can impersonal goods be relevant for distributive requirements? Take the case of national self-determination. Arguing against demanding global distributive requirements, nationalists claim that the self-determination or autonomy of national political societies is valuable in itself, and that principles regulating international affairs should respect national self-determination. The nationalist ideal is a world of self-governing societies where nations manage their own affairs in their own political society in accordance with their culture and way of life. The value of national self-determination underwrites a division of labour between domestic principles of distributive justice and principles regulating international affairs. Distributive justice should be the business of self-governing political communities. Principles regulating international affairs should serve to maintain background conditions in which self-governing political societies can flourish. Substantial international redistribution would not respect national self-determination as expressed in society's distributive choices, thus applying principles of distributive justice in the global domain is not desirable.[10]

The insight behind regarding national self-determination as impersonally good is that most people value certain kinds of relations in a manner that goes beyond their being instrumental to promoting the good of individuals. Proponents of the impersonal value of national self-determination see political bonds analogously. Social bonds in general and the relationship between citizens in political communities in particular are seen as valuable in themselves over and above their value as means to promoting the interests of individuals.[11] Because national self-determination is an impersonal good, it should be reflected in the way political communities relate to their members and to other political communities. Because this argument regards national self-determination as good impersonally, it is not concerned with the impact of self-determination on individual lives. The claim is not that membership in a self-determining nation makes one's life go better. This feature makes the impersonal version of the argument from national self-determination very problematic.

Liberals will object to viewing national self-determination as being impersonally valuable for the purpose of justifying requirements of distributive justice. They reject this view on the basis of the individualist moral universalism that is at the core of liberalism. The moral justification of actions, policies and institutions should consider the interests of individuals only. As members of communities, such as families or religious faiths, people might have conceptions of the good that regard their relations with fellow members as an impersonal good: for instance, they might believe that they ought to view family ties as good in themselves apart from the value they contribute to the lives of family members. Liberals argue, however, that political community should not be viewed like this for public justification. The principles that are supposed to guide the political organisation of society and the distribution of resources should be based on an impartial consideration of the good of individuals only. Political institutions determine citizens' rights and duties, and regulate and enforce the distribution of resources among persons with competing claims to them. It would be unfair for them to privilege any one conception of the good. While some might regard the life of someone devoted to participation in political life as good impersonally, not reducible to the value it contributes to individual well-being, it is inappropriate to organise political institutions and structure distribution in accordance with this view of political life. Doing so would amount to privileging one specific conception of the good over others under circumstances when people differ in their conceptions of the good. Thus, the justification of the content and scope of principles of justice should refer ultimately to individual lives and not suppose that 'society is an organic whole with a life of its own distinct from and superior to that of all its members in relation to one another' (Rawls 1999a: 234). States can make normative demands on individuals and on other states only if these demands can be justified with reference to the well-being of each individual concerned. A political regime cannot be a final end in itself; rather, it should be in place 'for the sake of individual human persons, who are the ultimate units of moral concern . . . Their well-being is the point of social institutions' (Pogge 1994: 210). In the face of the appeal of these considerations, the significance of people associating in communities with special obligations between them cannot simply be assumed to be foundational, without the need for justification (Kuper 2000: 652).

This normative individualist view applies to the justification of moral principles in general, and to principles of justice in particular. It is compatible, however, with viewing some goods as communal in the sense that their value presupposes membership in certain groups. For instance, some goods are culturally generated and might not be valuable outside the relevant culture. Access to the Internet may be regarded as a good in societies at a given level of technical development, possessing a culture that relies heavily on Internet-based communication and business.[12] Other cultures may not attach similar value to it. Many goods are thus generated by groups and must be viewed as communal rather than individual. National self-determination may be regarded as a communal good as well. The international political recognition of a nation and a right to participate in its political life are valuable to members only as members of a nation with which they identify. For someone who did not identify with a particular nation, its self-determination would be of no value. We have to distinguish, however, between communal goods and impersonal goods which have value beyond their value to individual persons. Even though the goods that need to be distributed may not be interpreted at the individual level, for normative purposes principles for justifying their distribution must ultimately take into account only the interests of individuals (Fabre 2007: 79). Viewing national community or culture as an impersonal good is unfair. These considerations give us a compelling reason to reject the version of the nationalist argument that is based on the impersonal value of national self-determination. It cannot justify the claim that there are no global requirements of justice nor can it show that, if such requirements exist, they are less demanding than obligations of justice to compatriots.

2.3.4 *National self-determination and individual well-being*

Finally, consider a reformulation of the nationalist argument from national self-determination that is compatible with individualism. We can give an individualist interpretation of the claim that the value of the political self-determination of nations warrants special domestic distributive requirements. This construal would be in line with the Rawlsian aspiration that 'we want to account for the social values, for the intrinsic good of institutional, community, and associative activities, by a conception of justice that in its theoretical basis is individualistic' (Rawls 1999a: 233–4). To the extent that collective entities have any moral importance, it is derivative, that is, it must be justified by reference to the interests of individuals. There are two strategies available for nationalists that are compatible with individualism.

The first strategy is to include communal self-determination among the goods individuals strive to attain. Some nationalists argue for the importance of national self-determination and the special distributive requirements it gives rise to by pointing out that people value participation in the public and civic life of their political society as well as being attached to their particular culture. National partiality is then justified because national identity is central to individual well-being and thus partiality to fellow nationals produces an important good. People prefer to govern their lives through communal decisions which enable them to develop and carry out special joint projects with their fellow nationals. Therefore, the world should consist of self-governing societies where nations manage their own affairs in their own political society in accordance with their culture and way of life.

We can spell out the argument in the following way. In line with individualism, political institutions should be justified by showing that they are conducive to individual well-being. Next, the argument assumes that national identity is constitutive of individual well-being. It follows, therefore, that political institutions should promote national identity. One can further assume that national self-determination, that is, political communities' right to make decisions about their communal good and life, is a necessary constituent of national identity. Therefore, political institutions should allow for national self-determination. Nationalists further argue that an important aspect of national self-determination so understood is national sovereignty over distributive matters. Because international redistribution would not respect the political autonomy of peoples, nationalists conclude, applying principles of distributive justice in the global domain is not desirable.

Is this argument convincing? The first two premises seem reasonable enough. Political institutions arguably should be conducive to individual well-being. Furthermore, for most people national identity is a constituent of well-being. One reason why this might be so is that national identity is important for people's self-respect. As Avishai Margalit and Joseph Raz argue, national or cultural groups are important because they provide 'an anchor for their [members'] self-identification and secure sense of belonging' (Margalit and Raz 1994: 133). That is, members' well-being is bound up with the flourishing of the national or cultural group with which they identify or belong. This can explain the point made by John Rawls, that is, that one function of political societies is to maintain their members' proper self-respect as participants in their society's history and culture (Rawls 1999b: 34).[13] Alternatively, David Miller argues that membership in a national community gives people a sense of belonging and also provides a background against which individuals can make choices about how to live their lives (Miller 1995: 85–6).

Granting these points, is the value of self-determination for members of political communities likely to justify the nationalist's restriction of the scope of principles of distributive justice to nation-states? The first thing to note is that ruling out international redistribution on grounds of the value of national distributive autonomy introduces considerations of a society's collective responsibility for its choices alongside the role played by national identity in individual well-being. As I will argue in Chapter 4, holding individuals accountable for the choices of the majority or governing elites of their societies is problematic. Furthermore, we must notice that this defence is a version of the instrumental case for national partiality we discussed earlier. The world's set-up of political institutions should leave room for national partiality because it is conducive to individual well-being, and therefore national partiality is desirable from an impartial perspective. Instrumental defences are problematic for the general reason noted earlier, however, and the argument from the value of national self-determination is vulnerable to a specific version of that criticism. It runs as follows. If political self-determination is an important means of preserving national identity that is in turn a constituent of individual well-being, everyone is presumed to have an equal claim to this good as well as to other goods that are important for other reasons. There are arguably, however, many other goods whose distribution among individuals is a matter of justice because they are also conducive to one's well-being. Because the instrumental approach requires that the interests of all individuals should be taken equally into account when justifying principles governing distribution, nationalists need to show that promoting one's well-being by self-determination through one's political society is so much more valuable for individuals than claims to other goods that it can override large international distributive inequalities. If they fail to show this, the value of political self-determination to inhabitants of a rich country cannot override claims of the global poor to a fair global distribution of income and wealth. Given the large current global differences in income and wealth, however, it would be a highly implausible assumption to make, and even nationalists themselves do not make it. If the value of political self-determination cannot override outsiders' distributive claims to other goods, it cannot rule out global distributive requirements.

The argument from the value of national identity is unlikely to justify the claim that there are no global distributive obligations; furthermore, it is implausible that obligations to our fellow nationals are significantly more demanding than what we owe to foreigners. Distributive principles serve other purposes besides leaving room for projects that promote individuals' well-being. For instance, they may have to secure individual rights and protect just entitlements. Thus, special requirements among compatriots allowing the pursuit of valuable joint projects are justified only when background justice obtains. Current international inequalities, however, and the lack of just global background institutions correcting for the unjust distributive effects of market transactions justify demanding global distributive obligations. Considerations of the good of self-determination figure as only one element in a theory of global justice, and they are unlikely to be strong enough to warrant strong priority to the interests of fellow nationals.

There is another route nationalists can take in their defence of national partiality on the ground of moral individualism. Instead of emphasising the value of national identity for individuals, some nationalists claim that special relationships can generate special distributive requirements because they produce goods which call for their own criteria of distribution. National partiality is justified because it concerns a special relationship among individuals which brings with it its own goods. The focus of this argument is not on the impartially desirable consequences of distributively autonomous special relations but on the division of benefits and burdens arising within these relationships.

Thomas Hurka has put forward a version of this argument for national partiality. He argues that nations are intrinsically valuable because fellow nationals as members of a scheme of political institutions are jointly creating some goods. To take one of his examples, Canadian identity is valuable because Canadians have created and maintained political institutions ensuring the rule of law, liberty and security of citizens, and also social security such as universal health care (Hurka 1997: 152–3). The common history of fellow nationals involved in the joint creation and provision of such goods constitutes a special relationship which is valuable and sufficient to justify differential distributive requirements among them (Hurka 1997: 152).

This account of the intrinsic value of special relationships among fellow nationals is problematic, however. To begin with, Hurka himself recognises that it blurs the distinction between membership in nations conceived as cultural communities and membership in nations as politically organised groups. These two types of relationship need to be distinguished, however: nations as political communities essentially embody a common set of laws and institutions regulating a system of cooperation, whereas nations conceived as cultural communities do not. Hurka's argument equivocates on two different meanings of the term 'nation', that is, nations as cultural communities and nations as groups of people subject to a common set of political institutions. The two kinds of relationship can generate special distributive requirements on different grounds. If we consider goods produced by participants in political institutions, distributive obligations owed by members to one another are not grounded in a special relationship they have with their *fellow nationals* but in the moral force of their special relationship with their *fellow citizens*. The force of Hurka's examples of the Canadian welfare system and the rule of law more plausibly comes from a conception of members as recipients of benefits of political cooperation, with an obligation of fair play as the grounding moral principle, or from conception of members as participants in, and subjects of, a just institutional scheme where the grounding principle is a duty to support and comply with just institutions. In either of these cases, the force of the argument, that we have obligations to the nation, derives from the fact that we are subject to institutions characterising politically embodied nations.[14]

If it is, indeed, cooperation regulated by political institutions that make nations intrinsically significant for justice, however, then it remains to be seen how political cooperation can justify partiality for fellow citizens. Hurka provides no argument from the political cooperation to a requirement of partiality to fellow citizens. Recently, there have been attempts to fill in the missing details in the argument and to justify special domestic distributive requirements on the basis of a relational account of distributive justice. The following two chapters will discuss arguments to justify special distributive demands among fellow citizens on the basis of the normative significance of political institutions applying to them.

2.4 SUMMARY AND CONCLUSION

This chapter looked at arguments by nationalists against the application of stringent principles of justice in the international domain. The first part described and rejected an argument against international justice that is based on Michael Walzer's relativistic view about justice. Walzer's theory regards the political institutions of nation-states as foundational in grounding requirements distributive justice insofar as they shape beliefs about distributive justice and set the framework within which social interpretation takes place. The refutation pointed out, first, that Walzer's thesis lacks empirical support because, on the one hand, it plays down the pervasiveness of intra-cultural disagreements about principles of justice and, on the other, it neglects the increasing reliance on norms of justice in international affairs. Second, Walzer's thesis is rejected as a normative position as well: Walzer's view about the relativity of social meanings of goods is biased towards certain conceptions of the good, and hence does not pay equal respect to the interests of individuals.

The second part of the chapter considered non-relativistic arguments for national partiality. It distinguished between instrumental and non-instrumental arguments. Instrumental arguments regard a global institutional structure, leaving room for national partiality, as instrumentally valuable from an impartial perspective whereas non-instrumental ones either point out some impersonal goods that arise in national political communities or regard political institutions of nation-states as representing a special relationship that is foundational in grounding special distributive requirements. I argued that instrumental arguments would have to rely on implausible assumptions if they wanted to establish the priority thesis. I further argued that non-instrumental arguments either would have to invoke a view of the impersonal value of national self-determination that is unacceptable to liberals or would need to provide a justification showing how the intrinsic goods produced by political communities are capable of justifying differential distributive claims by members in the face of conflicting claims by outsiders.

Notes

1 The argument draws on and modifies material from a previously published article (Miklós, 2009a).
2 Henry Shue introduced and argued against the thesis that 'compatriots take priority' (Shue, 1996, p. 132). The nationalist position I examine is a modified version of this view because, as I shall explain below, fellow nationals are not necessarily compatriots.
3 This characterisation follows the description made by Thomas Pogge in Pogge, 2002, p. 169.
4 Alisdair MacIntyre, Charles Taylor, Michael Sandel and Michael Walzer are perhaps the most prominent representatives of this relativistic stance (MacIntyre, 1985; Taylor, 1989; Sandel, 1982; Walzer, 1983).

5 Walzer offers an additional, normative, argument against the use of market exchange for the distribution of certain goods. He argues that, in liberal democratic societies, justice concerns numerous independent distributive spheres in which distribution should be determined by their own criteria. He considers market as one of these spheres but he claims that its role must be limited to the distribution of some kinds of goods. The danger Walzer sees in relying on market exchange for the distribution of a larger range of goods is that money has the tendency to become a dominant good, i.e. a good whose possession enables individuals having it to command a wide range of other goods the distribution of which is inappropriately sensitive to variations in individual wealth (Walzer, 1983, p. 22). Each of these goods, e.g. education, health care, food, Walzer thinks, should have its own distributive sphere, sufficiently insulated from money which should be confined to its own sphere and should not determine the distribution of other goods. The first thing to note about this argument is that, owing to the relativistic stance of Walzerian theory, it is valid only in liberal democratic cultures. It does not apply in caste societies, for instance, where the distribution of all goods is determined by one single distributive criterion, viz. one's position in the caste hierarchy. Second, as Jeremy Waldron argues, this account misrepresents the meaning of money even for liberal societies. Walzer is mistaken to regard money as a good, alongside other goods: money is only the 'representation of the commensurability of the meanings and values of other goods, not as a good with meaning or value in itself'. On the other hand, even though not a good, money does have a social meaning in liberal democratic societies, which is precisely that it can be exchanged to a whole range of goods (Waldron, 1995, p. 147). For this reason, it cannot be confined to its own sphere.

6 Unless otherwise specified, I use the term well-being in a broad sense, not denoting a welfarist view of distributive justice.

7 Dworkin argues that to value a product someone consumes in a manner that takes equal account of everyone's interests, we must measure the costs to others of his consuming this product, i.e. the 'cost in resources of material, labour, and capital that might have been applied to produce something different that somebody else wants' (Dworkin, 1985, p. 194).

8 Without endorsing nationalism, Samuel Scheffler provides the following characterisation. First, positive duties owed to fellow nationals are thought to be less easily overridden by considerations of cost to oneself than positive duties to citizens of other countries. Further, positive duties to fellow nationals are often thought to take precedence over one's positive duties to outsiders in case of conflict. Next, the threshold at which a positive duty can override a universal negative duty may be lower if the

positive duty is owed to a fellow national. On the other hand, the threshold at which a universal positive duty can override a negative duty can be higher if the negative duty in question holds with regard to fellow nationals (Scheffler, 2001, pp. 52–3).

9 Goodin does not argue for the nationalist thesis, however. He allows for cosmopolitan obligations at the fundamental level that place constraints on permissible national partiality.

10 David Miller argues that international redistribution similar in scope to that in liberal societies is ruled out because it would violate the value of the national self-determination of political societies (Miller, 1995, pp. 77–8)

11 This view of the good life is not identical with the conceptual point that some communitarians, such as Michael Sandel, make against liberalism, i.e. that liberalism rests on a mistaken view of the person, failing to see the importance of constitutive attachments in forming individual identity and interests (Sandel, 1982). The present claim is not so much about the conceptual incoherence of abstracting from particular attachments when justifying a conception of justice, as about the substantive content of this conception.

12 I owe this example to János Kis.

13 Rawls finds this function justified because, as he puts it, 'in this way belonging to a particular political society, and being at home in its civic and social world, gains expression and fulfillment' (Rawls, 1999b, p. 111).

14 See the argument made by Margaret Moore in Moore, 2001, pp. 36–7.

Chapter 3

THE POLITICAL CONCEPTION OF JUSTICE

The previous chapter concluded that nationalistic theories are unlikely to limit the scope of distributive justice to nation-states. The present chapter looks at an attempt to do so by showing that existing political institutions are fundamental for generating requirements of distributive justice. Unlike some arguments given by nationalists, this theory is individualistic about value; nonetheless, it holds that egalitarian distributive requirements apply only among citizens or residents of the same state. Rather than emphasising the value of national commitments in themselves or as means of attaining other valuable goods, it regards political institutions as a normatively significant relationship in which egalitarian distributive requirements obtain. Following our earlier characterisation, this is a relational conception that regards political institutions as necessary for the existence of requirements of justice. The requirement of equal treatment, and egalitarian distributive requirements that follow from it, do not obtain among individuals who are not tied together by common citizenship.[1] In this chapter, after a describing in detail an argument for this relational position about justice, I shall present some objections to it to show that this position is untenable as an account of egalitarian justice.

3.1 MAIN IDEAS

The political conception of justice holds that distributive justice is a specifically political virtue: its requirements emerge only in politically organised societies (Nagel 2005).[2] Governments should treat their citizens equally and accord them a fair share of resources as a matter of justice. The problem of justice is a political problem: it concerns how citizens ought to be treated by their government and what citizens owe

one another qua citizens. Political institutions create a special relationship between fellow citizens, and egalitarian distributive requirements
derive from this special relationship. This contingent and special moral
relation does not exist outside the bounds of political societies. It calls
for the application of special standards of equality within states. No
requirements of distributive justice apply across state borders, however.

The political conception of justice gives a particular answer to the
cosmopolitan intuition we started out with in this book. That intuition
stated that the life of a newborn in Mali is just as valuable as the life
of a newborn in Norway, and it is unfair that they face very different
life prospects. The sheer accident of someone's having been born in
Norway rather than in Mali should not make such a huge difference
to whether one can expect to live until the age of five or whether
one should expect to live one's life in dire poverty. Advocates of the
political conception deny that this inequality involves injustice. They
interpret distributive justice as applying only among fellow citizens
who are subject to the basic institutions of politically organised societies. The fact that large inequalities have a profound effect on people's
life prospects is not sufficient to explain the presumption against them.
An additional condition necessary to explain this presumption and the
requirement to justify any departure from the benchmark of equality
is that individuals should be members of the same society organised
along coercive political institutions.

What explains that it is only within a state that socio-economic
inequalities should be eliminated or mitigated? According to Thomas
Nagel, one of the main representatives of this position, requirements of
justice are based on the requirement of the equal treatment that sovereign states owe their citizens because they exercise 'comprehensive
control' over the framework of their citizens' lives (Nagel 2005: 123).
What makes political rule in states morally significant is that citizens
are subject to coercively imposed institutions that are collectively
authorised. It is this fact that generates special distributive demands
that do not exist outside the domain of coercive political institutions.
There are two crucial aspects of membership in political communities that Nagel thinks explain the requirement of equal treatment as
a demand of justice. First, all members are subject to coercive political
institutions that have a profound impact on their lives without their
consent. Through coercive institutions, the state issues directives
and applies them to all its citizens. These rules and directives deeply

influence the opportunities individual have from the start. Second, these coercive institutions are collectively authorised by all citizens. Collective authorisation involves the individual agency or will of members and it means the conjunction of two things. When states impose coercive rules on their citizens, they are not merely exercising power over them but normatively confer rights and impose duties on them. States claim authority and expect citizens 'to accept [the norms'] authority even when the collective decision diverges from [their] personal preferences' (Nagel 2005: 128–9). Furthermore, compliance with the legal system makes citizens 'joint authors' of the coercively imposed system of political institutions. The idea is that citizens are under an obligation to obey the law of their country and, at the same time, insofar as they uphold the law, they are held responsible for the imposition of a coercive legal system on fellow citizens. The two conditions, of having coercive political institutions with significant impact on people's lives and their joint authorisation by citizens, are necessary and jointly sufficient for the existence of the requirement of equal treatment and the egalitarian distributive requirements that follow from it.

In what sense can citizens be said to authorise a coercive legal system? The authorisation does not require a voluntary consent to the legal system on their part. Most of us have not voluntarily chosen to become or remain a member of our society. Nagel argues, however, that membership in a political community involves 'an engagement of the will that is necessary to live inside a society'. Citizens actively co-operate in upholding the legal system, otherwise the exercise of political authority over them would be pure coercion (Nagel 2005: 128–9). For citizens to authorise law it is sufficient if they actively comply with it and are expected to accept its authority. For example, we pay our taxes, we follow the current property law of the country when selling or buying goods, we write our wills in ways specified by law, and we are expected to do so *because* it is the law. By actively complying with their state's laws and accepting their authority, citizens are 'supporting the institutions through which advantages and disadvantages are created and distributed' (Nagel 2005: 129). Because we are implicated in upholding a coercive institutional scheme imposed on others, which has large material effects on their lives, we owe them a justification for the terms on which the scheme operates.

With the special relationship between citizens come special stand-

ards of justification. Consequential and coercive institutions and policies are regarded as representing the will of the citizenry without their
chance to give actual consent to them. If individual consent were a
viable option, as it is in voluntary associations, there would be no need
for providing justification to members beyond leaving for them the
opportunity to consent to political institutions and policies. The state
is no such voluntary association, however (Sangiovanni 2007: 17). It
makes political decisions binding all which we are required to obey,
and it requires us to take consequential responsibility for them even
when we disagree with their substance. The conjunction of involun-
tariness and collective authorisation calls for a special justification we
can demand from the state which is not required in the absence of this
special relationship between the state and its subjects. Because, without
having the choice to consent to authority we are held responsible for
the collective acts of the society, the state owes us a justification for the
substance of its social, political and legal institutions.

   Because individual consent is not an option, the justification must
take a different form. It must show that that the terms on which individuals cooperate under a government are reasonable from their point
of view. At the minimum, the justification must treat each person to
whom justification is owed – that is, each of us who is both subject to
coercive institutions and at the same time their authors – as an equal.
The requirement of equal treatment in turn gives rise to distributive
requirements that a country's scheme of institutions must meet. Nagel
argues that the appropriate form of justification that state institutions
and policies must satisfy is to show that they meet the requirements of
egalitarian justice. In particular, they secure political equality among
citizens, they provide for them equal opportunity to obtain desirable
positions and offices, and they reduce socio-economic inequalities that
arise among fellow citizens. The special status of citizens makes excep-
tional demands on them and brings with it special requirements that
state institutions must meet, that is, the requirements of distributive
justice (Nagel 2005: 130).

3.2 IMPLICATIONS FOR INTERNATIONAL DISTRIBUTIVE INEQUALITIES

What implications does the political conception have for the scope of
justice? The scope of the principles of justice depends on the scope of

the contingent special moral relation triggering the demand for justice. States have their boundaries and populations for various historical reasons but, given that they exercise sovereign power over their citizens, they must treat all their citizens equally and given that citizens are implicated in upholding the scheme of social, legal, and economic institutions of the state, they have special obligations to one another. Egalitarian requirements are owed by citizens of a state only to their fellow citizens (Nagel 2005: 121, 125).

The political conception in the form defended by Nagel leaves no room for requirements of global justice, when justice is understood in the egalitarian sense. Egalitarian distributive requirements within states were justified by an argument with a normative and an empirical premise. The normative premise was that the application of consequential coercive political institutions involving the will of their subjects is a necessary and sufficient condition for the existence of the requirement of equal treatment with respect to subjects and the egalitarian distributive requirements that follow from it. The empirical premise was that states comprise consequential coercive political institutions involving the will of their subjects, applying to all citizens. Defenders of the political conception, however, maintain the additional empirical point that, at the global level, there are no comparable coercive political institutions involving the will of their subjects. Because at present there are no coercive global political institutions capable of grounding full-blown requirements of justice at the global level, the issue of distributive justice does not arise globally. The requirements of distributive justice do not apply beyond nation-states.

The political conception's answer to the cosmopolitan intuition is this. The fact that the life expectancy at birth of a child born in Zimbabwe is about half that of a child born in Japan is certainly unfortunate and very plausibly a bad thing, but it is not unjust. There is no general requirement to reduce or eliminate inequalities in individual life prospects across the board. This requirement is generated only by the special relationship among fellow citizens. Therefore, the fact that the country where one is born significantly influences one's life prospects is not unjust because the difference between the relation of being fellow citizens and the relation of being fellow humans is morally relevant. Citizenship can legitimately determine one's life chances. An important caveat to add is that advocates of the political conception do not argue that there are no moral requirements applying across state borders. Nagel makes it explicit that there are pre-political rights and duties that do not depend on the existence of a state of which we are citizens. These rights and duties are pre-institutional in the sense that they bind us with regard to everyone in the world regardless of the presence or absence of institutional relations with them. Basic rights include human rights against violence, enslavement, coercion, rights to freedom of religion and expression (Nagel 2005: 127, 131). We might also have basic duties, such as the duty not to cause undue harm to others, and the humanitarian duties to rescue others from immediate danger and to provide assistance to the needy. It follows that, in the face of violations of human rights or severe deprivation afflicting the global poor, citizens of industrialised countries have duties regardless of the existence of a political relation with them.

The general idea behind this theory is that different principles are appropriate for regulating different domains. Morality is not unitary: principles that are valid for some domains are not appropriate for others. Different requirements may apply among citizens, among human beings and among political societies. Nagel holds that pre-political morality is relatively undemanding: basic moral rules require us not to violate the human rights of others and to provide basic humanitarian assistance such as rescue from immediate danger (Nagel 2005: 131). Basic rights and duties are part of this minimal morality that does not depend on any institutional relation between persons. Pre-institutional duties in the Nagelian picture are then gradually supplemented by additional obligations we may acquire in various ways, through various forms of voluntary and non-voluntary relations in which we stand with others.

This view of morality motivates Nagel's belief that some actions' or practices' having large material effects on people's lives are not sufficient to trigger the requirement of equal treatment that characterises a full conception of justice. Political relations matter for claims of justice. Nagel emphasises the example of immigration policies to illustrate his thesis. Immigration policies of affluent and powerful countries have an enormous impact on the lives of many people living in other countries but the political conception of justice does not see that as a reason for demanding that such policies should give the interests and opportunities of those others equal consideration (Nagel 2005: 129). The reason is that immigration laws do not expect would-be immigrants to accept their authority. They are simply enforced against them.

Nagel's account of the political conception of justice provides an original statement of a position that explains how we can have egalitarian duties that are not cosmopolitan but still compatible with moral universalism. Egalitarian demands are rooted in a universalistic associative duty: we have a duty to cooperate in according equal treatment to anyone with whom we are joined in a system of coercively imposed political institutions (Nagel 2005: 133). Egalitarian requirements are conditional: they are triggered only *once* we are fellow participants in a coercively imposed institutional scheme; we have no obligation to work towards equality-promoting institutions in the absence of a common political scheme. The link Nagel's political conception of justice establishes between political obligation and distributive egalitarian requirements, however, makes this account vulnerable to some objections. Nagel's political conception of justice offers an unsatisfactory account of both political obligation and the scope of distributive justice.

3.3 OBJECTIONS TO THE POLITICAL CONCEPTION OF JUSTICE

3.3.1 *The case of undemocratic states*

The first objection states that Nagel's political conception of justice is too restrictive in a way that makes it practically inapplicable to non-democratic regimes. The condition of collective authorisation that Nagel places on the applicability of the concept of justice to a scheme of political institutions requires that this scheme claims to be a 'collectively imposed social framework, enacted in the name of all those governed by it' (Nagel 2005: 140). This condition does not sit well with an important function any conception of justice should serve, namely that it should be a standard for criticising existing schemes. Many non-democratic regimes do not claim to impose their social framework on their subjects with their collective authorisation. Instead, they justify their rule with reference to divine will or divine right, or the good of a certain caste or group. In these cases, subjects are not even formally regarded as authors of the legal framework. Without a significant measure of rights to democratic participation, the claim that subjects are authors of the legal framework seems hard to justify. Arguably, the cooperation expected from subjects, and thus the involvement of their will, in such regimes fall short of what the political conception requires. When the regime cannot be said to be enacted with the authorisation of all the subjects, principles of justice would not serve as standards for criticism, which makes Nagel's account lack an important critical edge.[3] Analogously with the example of immigration law, the political conception would not have the resources to demand that the interests of subjects of tyrannical regimes be given equal consideration if laws are merely enforced on them, without asking for their acceptance (Nagel 2005: 129).

In response to this objection one might argue that it rests on a misunderstanding: the condition that political institutions are authorised by all subjects does not refer to the actual state of affairs but reflects a normative aim. For authority over subjects to be legitimate, it *should be* imposed on them with their authorisation. It is a normative requirement that authority must meet in order to be legitimate, and from this requirement follows the further one that the state should treat the interests of all subjects equally. If political institutions do not represent the will of subjects, political rule is open to the criticism that it is unjustified coercion. To make political authority legitimate, government must enact egalitarian policies and represent the will of all citizens. This defence is not open for Nagel, however. If institutions' collective authorisation by their subjects is not a necessary condition for the existence of egalitarian distributive obligations to them but a normative aim, the theory cannot limit the scope of justice to nation-states. Nagel's example of immigration law could no longer support his claim that policies or institutions with large material effects on people's lives ought to meet an egalitarian standard *only if* they are authorised by the subjects. After all, democratic states do not claim to make their immigration laws with the authorisation of would-be immigrants but neither are the domestic policies of some tyrannical regimes made with the authorisation of their subjects. Both cases involve institutions and policies with a significant impact on the lives of individuals, and in neither case are these made with the authorisation of the affected persons. So Nagel's account of political legitimacy and the political conception of justice faces a dilemma: either it is not the case that the authorisation of institutions by their subjects is a necessary condition of an egalitarian presumption about them, or the political conception is inapplicable to criticising undemocratic regimes as unjust.[4]

3.3.2 *Justifying political obligation and additional burdens*

The second objection to the political conception targets the conditions that seem sufficient in Nagel's account for grounding egalitarian duties of justice. One can argue that the conditions laid out in this conception are not sufficient to justify citizens' political obligation and the corresponding substantial distributive requirements. The political conception's account of political obligation is the following. The moral baseline of a requirement to respect basic rights and to provide humanitarian assistance can be exceeded by additional obligations people incur in various ways. A salient example of additional obligations is the case of voluntarily incurred obligations (Nagel 2005: 132). As compared to the minimal moral baseline, one is required to undertake more significant burdens if, for example, one has associated with others for a specific aim, or promised to perform some act. Even though these obligations may be more demanding than the minimal moral duties one owes to everyone else, we have nevertheless to perform them. Similarly, Nagel claims, the fact that we find ourselves under the authority of political institutions claiming our obedience in an involuntary association with others is sufficient to ground additional egalitarian obligations towards fellow citizens that we do not have to humanity in general (Nagel 2005: 132). By contrast, no matter how large the material effects that our actions have on the well-being of foreigners, we do not owe them more than the basic moral duties because they are not our associates in an involuntary political community.

One can object, however, that there is a contrast between voluntarily incurred special obligations and involuntary relations such as being fellow citizens of a state. In the first case, we can justify incurring obligations, in addition to a lower universal moral baseline, by pointing to our voluntary undertaking of them. No such justification is available in the case of political duties.[5] Many liberal theorists of political obligation argue that such additional obligations, which are usually associated with citizenship, cannot be justified on voluntaristic grounds (Simmons 1979). Nagel agrees with them in claiming that the nature of our special obligation to our fellow citizens is involuntary. If, however, we regard political obligation as involuntary, citizenship can ground additional (egalitarian) obligations toward fellow citizens only if we can give citizens a justification other than one based on voluntary consent. Political obligation and the corresponding additional distributive requirements are not normatively independent, that is, self-justifying (Simmons 1996: 266). The mere existence of a state cannot by itself create additional moral obligations for its subjects. There must be some prior moral principle that grounds these onerous obligations.

Nagel is aware that the justification of political obligation requires more than pointing out that citizens happen to find themselves in a common scheme of coercively imposed institutions. He conjectures that the duty to comply with political authority, and the move to a higher level of mutual obligations coming with it, may be based on 'a more basic obligation, emphasised by both Hobbes and Kant, that all humans have to create and support a state of some kind' which is, in turn, based on 'the imperative of securing basic rights' (Nagel 2005: 133). To secure basic rights, individuals have an obligation to work towards the establishment of common political institutions that are capable of providing assurance to individuals and coordinate their behaviour. Nagel argues that political obligation is not based on a universal requirement of equal treatment owed to all humans. The scope of the underlying requirement to secure basic rights of others is fuzzy, and the requirement can be met more or less locally (Nagel 2005: 133).

3.3.3 No obligation for foreigners to obey the law

Even if the political conception can succeed in justifying citizens' political obligation and the distributive requirements that go with it, it remains an inadequate account of political obligation. The next objection criticises the political conception by showing that it would lead to unacceptable implications for the obligations of foreigners. We saw that the requirement that citizens obey the laws of their country is necessary for them to demand equal treatment by their government. Furthermore, the coercive imposition of political institutions and the authorship of the law are jointly sufficient to generate full-blown requirements of egalitarian distributive justice. Nagel argues that, unlike citizens, foreigners cannot demand equal treatment because they are not subject to the requirement to obey the law which is a necessary aspect of our collective authorship of the law. Citizens are expected to uphold the law and to accept its authority even when some laws diverge from their preferences; foreigners are not, however. For this reason, fair equality of opportunity and the mitigation of socio-economic inequalities are not owed to foreigners. The fact that immigration laws have large material effect on the lives of prospective immigrants by itself generates no egalitarian distributive requirements. Because no obedience and acceptance are required of foreigners, immigration laws are a case of pure coercion from their perspective which need not be justified to them in the same way that the coercive imposition of laws on citizens must be justified (Nagel 2005: 129–30). The only justification foreigners can require is that immigration policies do not violate human rights or basic humanitarian obligations.

This position is subject to the following objection. Unless obedience to, and acceptance of, immigration laws are required of foreigners, these laws would have no moral force against them. Suppose an immigrant is attempting to enter the country illegally, violating some of its immigration laws. On Nagel's version of the political conception, states could not object to foreigners who refuse to obey their laws. Illegal immigrants could reply: 'We are not subject to the legal norms of the country the way citizens are. Unlike citizens, we are not required to accept and uphold the law. Since we have no duty to obey the immigration laws of your country, we do not commit anything wrong when we enter the country illegally.'

This argument shows that the joint conditions of subjection to coercive laws, as well as a duty to comply with them, cannot have the make-or-break significance for distributive justice Nagel attributes to it. If it did, Nagel would face a dilemma. He can maintain that foreigners are required to comply with immigration laws, in which case they can rightly be regarded as authors of these laws. Because immigration laws are coercive institutions with profound impact on the lives of immigrants, the requirement to obey them and to accept their authority is sufficient for the existence of egalitarian distributive requirements. This requirement would apply in the case of foreigners as well. Alternatively, Nagel would have to agree that states cannot object to foreigners refusing to comply by invoking their duty to obey the law. This response would conflict with the right states typically claim against foreigners to prohibit and control movement across their borders and immigration which is one of the standard features of territorial states.

The political conception does not provide an adequate account of political obligation. It purports to show that common citizenship is both necessary and sufficient to generate an obligation to obey the law and corresponding egalitarian distributive requirements, and has the implication that these requirements do not arise in the case of foreigners. It cannot account for the obligation of foreigners to obey the law, however, without at the same time granting that the state owes egalitarian distributive obligations to them.

3.3.4 *Injustice against outsiders*

Not only is it plausible to think that foreigners have a duty to accept just laws that apply to them but it is also likely that citizens and the government, in turn, have duties of justice to foreigners beyond basic humanitarian ones. The political conception is subject to the further objection that it tolerates injustice to outsiders. After all, it permits unequal treatment and large socio-economic inequalities across borders which we would consider unjust if they took place within the state's borders. We saw that Nagel regards this objection as misguided because, by construction, requirements of justice apply only among fellow citizens subject to the same set of political institutions. Outsiders have no claims of justice against government and citizens.

The political conception gives an implausible account of the distributive obligations that states have to outsiders, however. Political institutions can be unjust in the manner in which they treat foreigners as well as citizens. I will describe three examples to support the claim that domestic institutions and policies can be unjust in the way they treat outsiders.

First, following the logic of Nagel's political conception, states have egalitarian obligations to outsiders because they enforce coercive laws against them and expect foreigners to accept and obey them. The treatment of outsiders by domestic institutions must be evaluated by standards of justice in a broad range of cases owing to the territorial nature of governance that characterises states. As the immigration example showed, states comprise coercive institutions with a profound impact on the lives of foreigners. The example emphasises a general feature of the state system that calls for justification. By carving out a jurisdiction for themselves, territorial states unilaterally subject outsiders to their coercive control insofar as they deny or restrict the freedom of the latter to move into their domain, to obtain private property and to engage in economic activities there. They claim the right to deny or to restrict access for outsiders to their territory and to the resources within their territory. These rules have a significant impact on the lives of foreigners. Furthermore, states exercise coercive power against foreigners when carrying out these functions. Insofar as foreigners are expected to obey and accept these coercive institutions, they are owed a justification for the content of the rules. Political institutions are subject to justice-based evaluation from the vantage point of outsiders as well. The logic of Nagel's political conception of foreigners compels us to conclude that foreigners are owed egalitarian distributive requirements of justice.

Next, states may be subject to some egalitarian requirements vis-à-vis foreigners owing to their institutions' and policies' substantial impact on foreigners' lives. One can argue that states are required to enforce formal equality of opportunity requirements in the relationship between their subjects and foreigners. Imagine the following scenario. A company is recruiting employees from abroad for work at a manufacturing plant in the home country. In their employment policies they systematically favour men over women. Of equally qualified male and female job candidates, they always pick men over women, and of equally qualified employees, they are much more likely to promote men. Suppose further that this discrimination is not against the law of the country where the corporation is based. Nagel's argument would imply that there is nothing unfair or unjust about this. Equal opportunity in employment is not a requirement applying to the relationship between the corporation and foreigners or to the relationship between the government and foreigners. Even if we regard the preferential treatment of male over female citizens as unfair, the requirement of equal opportunity in hiring and promotion does not apply with regard to outsiders.

This position is implausible, however. If it is unfair for one agent to discriminate against women from the corporation's home country, by the same token it seems unfair for the same agent to discriminate against women from abroad. Note that the objection holds for all other forms of discrimination we regard as unjust in the case of citizens: for instance, racial discrimination seems no less unfair when it is targeted against foreign nationals. If we accept that the principle of non-discrimination is a requirement of socio-economic justice, at least this aspect of socio-economic justice is bound to have a global scope because state borders seem to be irrelevant for non-discrimination on grounds of race or gender. States then owe some egalitarian distributive obligations to foreigners by virtue of the fact that they apply consequential rules to them.

Finally, some further requirements of distributive justice – though

not necessarily egalitarian requirements – can follow from the consequential impact of domestic institutions and policies on the lives of outsiders. In particular, international interdependence – when collective
actions taken by people in different parts of the world mutually have an
impact on the lives of people elsewhere – can generate requirements
of distributive justice that go beyond basic humanitarian requirements.
Consider the case of medical brain drain. Studies have shown that
health outcomes in many poor countries have been negatively affected
by health worker migration (Eyal and Hurst 2008; Daniels 2008). This
migration has been going on in large scale in the last decades, with
a significant effect on the health status of citizens of poor countries.
Between 23 and 34 per cent of physicians in developed countries are
foreign trained, and a substantial proportion of this figure is made up
of physicians migrating from developing countries. For example, over
60 per cent of doctors trained in Ghana in the 1980s have emigrated,
as a result of which 47 per cent of physicians' posts (and 57 per cent of
nursing posts) were unfilled in 2002 (Daniels 2008: 330). The effects of
this migration on poor-country health outcomes have been very significant because these countries find it increasingly difficult to carry out
basic public health functions. Policies aimed at improvements in health
status are sometimes hindered by the lack of qualified health personnel
in the target areas. Most parts of Africa have to rely on one to two physicians per 100,000 population to carry out basic health care functions
whereas, in the United States, there are 188 physicians per 100,000
(Daniels 2008: 330; Eyal and Hurst 2008). Because the migration of
health workers contributes to better health outcomes in better-off
countries, while leaving the health status in countries of origin worse, it
contributes to international health inequalities.

It has been noted that the causes of brain drain are not entirely – and
arguably not even primarily – endemic to sending countries: the policies of receiving countries play a large role. Receiving countries have
pursued aggressive recruitment strategies to fill quickly health care
posts left open by their educational systems. Thus, demand in receiving
countries is shaped by a large-scale government-coordinated policy
which makes it difficult for the sending countries to counter its adverse
effects (Daniels 2008: 330). These factors contributing to medical brain
drain undermine Nagel's point that states are immune from considerations of distributive justice vis-à-vis outsiders, subject to the constraint
of respecting human rights and basic humanitarian obligations (Nagel

2005: 130). This seems implausible, however, given the fact that policy decisions a country makes about training health personnel and about access to its territories have a substantial impact on the life prospects of people living in other countries, and vice versa. There is interdependence between the institutions and policies of different countries.

Joshua Cohen and Charles Sabel argue that interdependence produces requirements of justice that go beyond basic humanitarian requirements. These requirements may be procedural, such as the requirement that subjects be included in the decision-making procedure affecting their fundamental interests, or substantive, such as giving priority to the basic needs of the poorest or egalitarian distributive requirements (Cohen and Sabel 2006: 169).

To sum up: states owe obligations of justice to foreigners owing to the consequential impact of their institutions and policies – which may or may not be coercively enforced – on foreigners' lives. Standards of justice for evaluating the relationship between states and outsiders can range from procedural rules, demanding the inclusion of foreigners in decision-making mechanisms, to substantive distributive requirements.

3.3.5 Unjust global institutions

Injustice by domestic institutions to outsiders is one instance where cross-border considerations of justice arise. There is another case, too, which motivates our final objection to the political conception. Besides domestic institutions, global institutions can also give rise to requirements of justice applying across state borders.

We saw that the political conception regards coercive political institutions involving the will of their subjects as a necessary condition of requirements of distributive justice. It also makes the empirical point that, at the global level, there are no comparable institutions, and it concludes that no distributive requirements arise there beyond basic humanitarian obligations. Both the empirical and the normative points can be criticised. In what follows I will show that:

1. there are coercive political institutions at the global level sufficient to generate requirements of distributive justice, and also that
2. considerations of distributive justice can arise apart from coercive political institutions, and they, indeed, arise globally.

The empirical premise can be criticised along the following lines. Arguably, there are some supranational institutions with substantial impact on individual interests that are coercive and that involve the will of these people. Supranational institutions are relevantly similar to domestic political institutions. Consider two reasons why Nagel thinks that no obligations of justice arise in the international domain. First, he regards supranational institutions as the products of mutually beneficial intergovernmental agreements that are fully voluntary and are unlike the coercive institutions of states. The normative requirements that fully voluntary agreements, such as 'pure contracts', and intergovernmental agreements generate are entirely conventional: their content is exhausted by the terms of the agreements. The relationships between parties themselves generate no new norms.[6] Nagel argues that the norms of egalitarian justice are not conventional in this sense: their content is defined by an independent requirement of justice that is triggered in the special relationship within a state, independent of voluntary undertakings. The other reason why Nagel thinks states differ from supranational institutions is that he sees a sharp contrast between the way the two kinds of institution relate to individuals. The relationship between the government and citizens is always direct, with the government directly interpreting, applying and enforcing rules over citizens. By contrast, Nagel argues that the relationship between supranational institutions and individuals is indirect. Interpretation and enforcement of rules is always mediated by member-state governments. Nagel thinks this is illustrated by the fact that citizens direct their complaints against their own governments, rather than against supranational bodies, for accepting supranational agreements.

This characterisation of the international system is incorrect, however. The relationship between supranational institutions and individuals is both non-voluntary and direct. As Joshua Cohen and Charles Sabel argue, opting out of some supranational institutions, such as the International Monetary Fund (IMF) or World Trade Organization (WTO), is not a real option for member countries and their citizens (Cohen and Sabel 2006: 168). Non-compliance with, or exit from, these organisations are prohibitively costly for most member states, especially for less powerful ones, which arguably amounts to coercion because non-compliance is subject to severe sanctions.[7] Not only are supranational institutions coercive against governments, they also coerce individuals. Cohen and Sabel show that there is a direct rule-making relationship between some supranational institutions and the individuals subject to them: organisations such as the IMF and WTO have a de facto decision-making independence from member-country governments when they make, specify and apply rules (Cohen and Sabel 2006: 165). Owing to this direct relationship, they coercively impose rules on individuals even when they lack their own independent enforcement powers. They fundamentally shape individual conduct by providing incentives and permitting the imposition of sanctions in a growing number of areas, such as food-safety standards, product standards, labour standards and environmental regulation.

Furthermore, the wills of individuals are implicated in these rules just as they are in domestic institutions. Supranational directives have a legally binding force, and domestic legislation must be made pursuant to them. By complying with domestic rules that were made following supranational directives, citizens actively cooperate in upholding the supranational institutional system.

This argument refutes both of Nagel's claims. International institutions are not like fully voluntary agreements nor are international rules necessarily mediated by member-state governments. International institutions are relevantly similar to domestic ones.

To summarise: even if we accept Nagel's description of the characteristics that generate egalitarian requirements of justice – that is, coercive institutions with large material impact on people's lives which citizens are both subject to and authors of – Nagel's conclusion does not follow because he gets wrong the *scope* of institutions that have these characteristics and thus the scope of egalitarian justice.

The argument against the global application of considerations of justice can also be criticised by rebutting the normative premise of the argument. One can argue that some considerations of justice – though not necessarily egalitarian distributive requirements – can arise even outside coercive political institutions involving the will of their subjects. I shall describe three cases when – *pace* Nagel – supranational institutions can be subject to requirements of justice. International relationships involving cooperative schemes, global institutions harming the poor, and agencies responsible for the distribution of a particular good can all be seen as generating either procedural or substantive requirements of distributive justice. Justice requires that subjects in these relationships be included in making decisions that significantly affect them. Justice can also demand that the interests of the worst off be given more weight than the interests of the better off, or that the most urgent needs should be satisfied if it can be done at relatively little cost to others. At the limit, obligations of equal treatment can arise in these relationships and generate egalitarian distributive requirements (Cohen and Sabel 2006: 154).

Consider first international cooperation through supranational institutions. Cohen and Sabel argue that the relation of institutionally governed cooperation generates requirements of justice internationally, possibly ranging from obligations of inclusion to those of equal treatment, going beyond humanitarian considerations. For example, the current global intellectual property rights regime enacted in the TRIPs agreement (Agreement on Trade-Related Aspects of Intellectual Property Rights) can quite plausibly be regarded as a case of mutual cooperation governed by a set of rules. It significantly affects research and development in the pharmaceutical industry by providing incentives that allow pharmaceutical companies temporary monopoly on their new products. Furthermore, the scope of cooperation is global in which subjects of member countries follow, and are expected to follow, the rules of cooperation. The current international patent regime has been criticised for leading to a neglect of diseases that are typically endemic in poorer countries, and for concentrating resources on developing drugs for diseases characteristic of wealthier countries. Most newly developed drugs tend to reduce the global burden of disease to a much more limited extent than drugs targeting some neglected diseases could potentially do. Drugs for these remain undeveloped, however, because of the lack of purchasing power in poor countries.[8] Those at the bottom receive no or very little benefit from the scheme even though they are required to abide by the terms of cooperation. At the same time, residents of affluent countries greatly benefit from the drugs whose development was made possible by the existing regime. For this reason, Thomas Pogge argues that the current regime contributes to health inequalities between the rich and poor worldwide (Pogge 2010).

The asymmetry in research and development could be mitigated or eliminated by substituting or supplementing the current intellectual property rights regime with a different set of rules providing greater incentives for the development of drugs targeting diseases that afflict the poor (Pogge 2010). Such a scheme could greatly benefit the poorest at little cost to those who benefit the most from the current scheme.

The precise details of the new regime can be left open for the purposes of this argument.[9] What is important to note is that pharmaceutical research and development is a clear case of international rule-governed cooperation with pervasive effects on the life prospects of people. It has significant implications for health outcomes and their distribution. The current form of cooperation provides very little benefit to the poorest but there are available alternative schemes that could much better meet the basic health needs of the worst off while not requiring a lot of sacrifices from the affluent. Arguably, international cooperative schemes with substantial impact on individual life prospects can generate requirements of justice, for example in the form of greater inclusion in decision-making mechanisms or giving priority to the interests of the worst off (Daniels 2008).

The second attempt to justify international requirements of justice is based on the harmful impact of supranational institutions. Thomas Pogge argues that citizens of affluent countries owe substantial distributive obligations to the global poor as a matter of justice because they have been harming them through global institutions. Pogge distinguishes between positive duties to assist the needy and negative duties, such as the duty not to cause undue harm to others. Because westerners are implicated in upholding the global economic order that harms the global poor, Pogge argues, we have violated a negative duty and owe the impoverished the duty to rectify the injustice (Pogge 2002).

Whether or not this argument is sound depends both on the normative point about how to interpret the notion of harm that plays a key role in the argument and also on the truth of Pogge's empirical claim that the global economic order has harmed the poor. The claim that the global institutional order has harmed the poor presupposes that the poor have fared worse than a relevant baseline as a result of the causal impact of global institutions. To determine whether harm has been done, we can rely on a historical baseline and compare how the poor are doing compared with their position at some earlier time, or we can employ a hypothetical baseline and determine whether the poor are better or worse off relative to a state of nature where there is no institutional interaction at the global level. Whereas it seems impossible to assess the claim that the global poor are worse off than they would be in the absence of global institutions, Pogge and others disagree about whether the global order has harmed the poor in comparison with their position at an earlier time. International institutions have arguably brought about benefits as well as harms for the poor: for example, the global pharmaceutical intellectual property rights regime has benefited the poor through the spread of more affordable generic drugs relying on the ingredients of drugs developed under the protection of intellectual property regime (Daniels 2008: 332). Though, as we saw, the existing regime is not optimal because it neglects the needs of the poorest, its benefits may have considerably improved the lives of at least some of the poor.[10] If, however, it can be shown that the global order has harmed *some of* the poor while it benefited others, citizens of affluent countries who contribute to this harm have an obligation to rectify it. This obligation would be compatible with the premises of Nagel's political conception but would undercut his conclusion that there are no obligations of socio-economic justice at the global level. Assuming we may have obligations of distributive justice owing to our violation of our duty not to cause undue harm to others, the existence of global institutions can generate requirements of justice that go beyond humanitarian duties, though the extent of these duties would probably fall short of the egalitarian obligations citizens owe one another.

Finally, the third example of supranational institutions generating requirements of justice concerns supranational agencies responsible for distributing basic goods such as education and health care. Take the World Health Organization (WHO) which is responsible for distributing public health expertise and technology. If the WHO systematically ignored the health needs of a particular group of people in its member countries while favouring others, this would be regarded not merely as a violation of its mission to promote world health but also unjust. To give an example, concerns about the fair distribution of health benefits arise in discussions about the distribution of antiretroviral therapies against HIV/AIDS. The underlying tenor of these discussions is that the WHO must treat equally the interests of all when deciding about the distribution of goods it is responsible for (Daniels 2008: 344). This demand is identical to what the political conception attributes to coercive political institutions and invokes considerations of justice.

All the three cases discussed in this section can give rise to requirements of distributive justice. They do not represent the non-relational view of justice, however. What makes international inequalities unjust is not independent from the special relations we stand in with others in other countries. Nor do these cases regard the mere fact of an agent having large material impact on the lives of others as sufficient to generate obligations of justice. All these cases are compatible with the relational view of justice because they all describe a particular rule-governed relation that generates requirements of justice. They emphasise the institutional relations of cooperative schemes, harm through institutions and agencies responsible for the distribution of a particular good. They go beyond the political conception in that they acknowledge other morally significant relations besides coercive political institutions of sovereign states that can be evaluated by principles of justice.

To conclude, the political conception of justice is wrong about the scope of considerations of justice because it fails to take account of institutional relations at the global level that can generate requirements of justice. At the global level, there are both coercive political institutions, relevantly similar to domestic ones, and other kinds of relationship that can give rise to requirements of justice.

3.4 SUMMARY AND CONCLUSION

The chapter looked at a further strand of theories that deny the existence of global requirements of justice. Unlike the nationalist arguments against global justice reviewed in the previous chapter, which rely on a relativistic view of justice or emphasise the value of national commitments in themselves or as means to attaining other valuable goods, this position regards the political institutions of sovereign nation-states as a normatively significant special relationship that is necessary for the requirements of distributive justice. The chapter focused on the political conception of justice, which attempts to derive egalitarian requirements of distributive justice from the need to justify the use of coercive force by states against their subjects regardless of their consent, and subjects' obligation to obey political decisions. This defence of egalitarian justice is based on the special significance of coercive institutions with substantial impact on people's lives and on a collective view of moral agency grounding the collective authorship of the state's distributive decisions by members of the political community. The political conception tries to draw a principled distinction between the institutions of sovereign states capable of generating egalitarian requirements within political societies and the global domain where we can find only basic humanitarian requirements. I have argued against this conception by making five objections showing that it is problematic as an account of political obligation, and it is also mistaken about the scope of distributive justice.

It fails on both counts since:

1. it cannot criticise undemocratic states.

   It is an inadequate account of political obligation because:

2. it has difficulties establishing that citizens have an obligation to obey the law and
3. it has the implication that foreigners have no obligation to obey immigration laws.

   The political conception also gets wrong the scope of justice because:

4. it permits injustice against outsiders and
5. fails to consider various ways global institutions can be unjust.

Thus, the political conception cannot successfully limit the scope of requirements of justice to nation-states.

Notes

1 I leave open several questions that must be answered by egalitarian theories of distributive justice. For instance, I do not discuss the question about the distribuendum, i.e. what it is that should be distributed equally. Candidates for equalisation in the literature have included welfare, resources, primary goods, capabilities, opportunity for welfare, and access to advantage. Nor do I aim to settle debates about the conditions on the basis of which inequality should be permitted.
2 Similar accounts with different emphases have been defended by Blake (2001), Risse (2005b) and Miller (1998).
3 See the arguments by Cohen and Sabel (2006, pp. 160–1) and Julius (2006, pp. 180–1).
4 Attila Tanyi has suggested to me that one can regard immigrants as having authorised the laws of the receiving country, including its immigration laws. In response, there are two things to note. First, it would then follow that all immigrants within a state's territory – including illegal ones – would be owed full-blown egalitarian obligations that are due to citizens because they are subject to coercive laws which they have authorised. Second, the objection against Nagel would still hold because states' laws cannot be said to be authorised by would-be immigrants who are excluded from their territory.

5 This is the tenor of Samuel Scheffler's Voluntarist Objection to associative obligations (Scheffler, 2001, pp. 54, 70).

6 Private contracts among fellow citizens are not like this, Nagel argues, because they rely on a complex web of prior rules, such as property and tax law, that are meant to make sure that the socio-economic system remains just. Pure contracts and international agreements, by contrast, contain no assurance that just background conditions obtain and generate no obligations to secure background justice.

7 Without offering a precise definition of coercion, I follow Alan Wertheimer's description. An agent A coerces an agent B to do X only if A threatens to make B worse off with reference to some baseline condition if B chooses not to do X (Wertheimer, 2008, p. 75).

8 This phenomenon is termed the 10/90 gap, a shorthand for the claim that only about 10 per cent of the funding in global pharmaceutical research and development is targeted at diseases accounting for 90 per cent of the global disease burden. Even if the ratio is, in fact, better, R & D funding for diseases afflicting the poor is still disproportionately low.

9 Notable recent proposals include Michael Kremer's Advance Market Commitments and Thomas Pogge's Health Impact Fund (Kremer and Glennerster, 2004; Pogge, 2010).

10 See Mathias Risse's argument against Pogge along these lines (Risse, 2005a).

Chapter 4

RAWLSIAN JUSTICE AND THE
LAW OF PEOPLES

Having reviewed political theories of justice, I shall now turn to another representative of relational theories denying the existence of global requirements of egalitarian justice. Just like the political conception of justice, this view regards the political institutions of nation-states as necessary to generate egalitarian requirements. Unlike the political conception, however, the position reviewed in this chapter emphasises other features of political institutions besides their coercive exercise of power over citizens and citizens' collective authorisation of political coercion. I focus on the work of John Rawls who laid out a very influential position on domestic distributive justice but who, in subsequent work, denied the existence of requirements of egalitarian distributive justice at the global level. I begin by outlining some main elements of the egalitarian theory of justice set forth by Rawls. I describe the problem of social justice as Rawls understands it, and on the conditions necessary for grounding requirements of justice in the Rawlsian theory. I then proceed by presenting Rawls's views about the nature and justification of principles for regulating the conduct of international affairs as developed in his *The Law of Peoples*, focusing on some of his major objections to global requirements of distributive justice. Having done so, I argue against Rawls's reasons for rejecting the demand for international distributive justice by pointing out their lack of factual support and inconsistency with the main tenets of the liberal egalitarian theory of justice Rawls defends in his earlier work.

4.1 RAWLS'S DOMESTIC THEORY OF JUSTICE

John Rawls provided the most systematic and most influential account of social justice in the twentieth century. Before considering the implications of his work for global justice, it is necessary to give a brief summary of Rawls's domestic theory of justice. Rawls develops his theory of justice for domestic societies in *A Theory of Justice* and in *Political Liberalism*. Rawlsian justice is an example of what we have called the relational view of justice. I described the relational view earlier as holding that individuals' standing in a specific practice-mediated relation is a necessary condition for requirements of distributive justice to exist among them. For Rawls, the relevant practice-mediated relation is the relation between fellow participants in a system of social cooperation: Rawlsian justice is concerned with regulating social cooperation among individuals. The scope of justice is then limited to those individuals who are fellow participants in a scheme of social cooperation: justice is a property of schemes of social cooperation. The problem of justice is to formulate principles in accordance with which benefits and burdens from social cooperation get distributed in a fair manner. Requirements of justice, then, should determine the distribution of benefits and burdens that result from schemes of social cooperation. What sort of cooperation is Rawls's theory concerned with? Rawls is interested in cooperation that is regulated by the basic institutions of society, or what he calls the basic structure. More precisely, the basic structure is 'the way in which the major social institutions distribute fundamental rights and duties and determine the division of advantages from social cooperation' (Rawls 1999a: 6). Rawls argues that principles of distributive justice apply only in the context of social cooperation within the basic structure. They do not apply in other contexts, however (Rawls 1999a: 6–7; Rawls 1993: 261; Rawls 2001: 10–11).

Why is Rawls's theory focused on the way the basic structure regulates social cooperation? The main reason Rawls gives is that the basic structure has profound effects on the life prospects of individuals subject to it (Rawls 1999a: 7). Rawlsian justice is not concerned with trivial benefits and costs resulting from social interaction; its focus is on those benefits and burdens of social cooperation that decisively shape individuals' lives. People born into different social positions have different expectations of life; they have different opportunities, different goals and different skills, and these inequalities are present from the start. Socio-economic inequalities are to a large extent the product of the working of political, social and economic institutions comprising the basic structure. The basic structure exerts its profound impact on life prospects by shaping the aims and aspirations people have, by influencing the development and realisation of individual talents and abilities, and by permitting significant social and economic inequalities in the life prospects of individuals, 'depending on their social origins, their realised natural endowments, and the chance opportunities and accidents that have shaped their personal history' (Rawls 1993a: 270).[1] Such fundamental inequalities in life prospects call for regulation by justice.

Requirements of justice obtain between those who are fellow participants in this consequential basic structure. When just, the basic structure regulates interactions among individuals such that it secures and preserves the fairness of social cooperation. Rawls argues that interpersonal agreements are morally acceptable only if they are made freely, under conditions that are fair (Rawls 1993a: 266). Excessive social and economic inequalities work against the fairness of social conditions. Without the basic structure maintaining an equal measure of basic rights, liberties, and opportunities, and a fair distribution of resources, interpersonal agreements will not have been freely made under fair circumstances. The basic structure performs this function by appropriately regulating and adjusting background conditions in a way that precludes large differentials in bargaining power and prevents social relations from mapping the distribution of inequalities in social and natural resources. The institutions of the basic structure are essential for maintaining the fairness of social and economic processes because, even if individual transactions are fair when considered in isolation, the cumulative effects of an indefinite series of such fair transactions will be unjust (Rawls 1993a: 266). Institutions are much more effective in securing background justice.

Principles of justice provide the standard of fairness by which social cooperation should be evaluated. Rawls argues that the allocation of the benefits and burdens of social cooperation should be governed by two principles of justice. The first of these stipulates that everyone has an equal right to basic liberties such as liberty of conscience, freedom of association, freedom of movement, and so on. The second principle demands that people should enjoy fair equality of opportunity to obtain valuable positions and offices, and requires that socio-economic inequalities should be to the benefit of the worst-off members of society (Rawls 1999a: 53; Rawls 1999a: 72).

Rawls argues for his two principles of justice as follows. Fair principles of distributive justice are those that individuals would choose as a contractual agreement in a hypothetical situation that Rawls calls the original position. We should imagine that parties in the original position rationally choose principles of justice on the basis of their self-interest but they are denied knowledge of their social background, their talents and skills, as well as their ideas about how to lead their lives. As Rawls puts it, parties are behind a 'veil of ignorance' that excludes parties' knowledge of their conceptions of the good, their social standing such as their 'class position or social status', and their endowment with natural assets such as intelligence or strength (Rawls 1999a: 11). The contract that parties would agree to under these circumstances produces fair principles of justice because people are unable to choose principles that systematically advantage their personal interests. We have different ideas about how to lead our lives; we differ in our talents and skills; and we come from different social backgrounds. Allowing us to choose principles in full knowledge of all this information would be wrong for two reasons. First, Rawls thinks the distribution of goods should not be allowed 'to be improperly influenced' by morally contingent or arbitrary factors, such as sex, race, the social class of their parents, and their inborn natural endowments (Rawls 1999a: 62–3). These morally contingent differences between people should not be used to justify principles of justice. Second, Rawls stipulates that we are autonomous agents capable of framing, revising and pursuing a conception of the good life. If we were to know what idea of a good life we want to pursue, we would choose principles of justice that allow us to exercise rights and freedoms important to us at the expense of rights and freedoms important to others (Rawls 1999a: 16–7). Fairness, however, requires that principles of justice do not take into account these contingencies. Thus, in the hypothetical situation of the original position, parties know that they have differential abilities and pursue different goals but they do not know what particular abilities and goals they have. They also know how the social organisation they will choose will affect the degree to which individuals with particular abilities are likely to reach certain kinds of goals. Finally, the choice of goods to be distributed would need to avoid bias towards any particular conception of the good. Thus, rather than thinking about how to distribute particular goods, parties decide about distributing social primary goods, that is, goods that every rational person is presumed to want: rights and liberties, income and wealth, opportunities and powers, and the social bases of self-respect. Under this radical uncertainty, parties would choose principles of justice that benefit the worst off because they could not tell whether they will themselves end up in the worst-case scenario, and they would want to avoid being put in an unnecessarily bad position. They would want to maximise the prospects of the worst off as measured in their share of primary goods. That is, they would choose a set of institutions that secure an expansive set of rights and arrange material inequalities in a way that favours the poorest.

Rawls argues that parties would adopt two principles of justice.

First principle: each person is to have an equal right to the most extensive scheme of equal basic liberties compatible with a similar scheme of liberties for others (Rawls 1999a: 53).

Second principle: social and economic inequalities are to be arranged so that they are, (a) to the greatest expected benefit of the least advantaged, and (b) attached to offices and positions open to all under conditions of fair equality of opportunity (Rawls 1999a: 72).

These principles do not demand a strictly equal distribution of primary goods. They allow for inequalities in society just in case they maximally benefit the worst-off members of society. For example, unequal incomes in society are justified if they are necessary to attract talented people to work in productive jobs and to exert maximal effort, because part of the surplus thus created would benefit the poorest. More wealth will be available for society as a result of this incentive, and government can redistribute part of it such that the poor end up better off than they would be under a completely equal distribution. Because, however, I rely on a broad understanding of egalitarianism in this book which requires the reduction of socio-economic inequalities, I shall treat these principles as egalitarian because they considerably limit the range of permissible socio-economic inequalities.

4.2 RAWLS'S LAW OF PEOPLES

4.2.1 *Justifying the Law of Peoples*

Rawls's two principles of justice would radically limit socio-economic inequalities. But what is the scope of these principles? Do they apply globally? In his subsequent work, Rawls denies this. He argues that the application of egalitarian requirements of justice is limited to nation-states and that only limited distributive obligations arise at the inter-national level. In the remaining part of this chapter I evaluate Rawls's own ideas of extending the scope of his theory to the global domain as they are presented in his later book, *The Law of Peoples* (Rawls 1999b).[2] This monograph offers a discussion of a broad array of issues covering subjects from the justification of human rights to the morality of war to the ethics of statesmanship. The argument is a significant modification and elaboration of Rawls's brief remarks about 'the law of nations' in *A Theory of Justice*.[3] In the following section I shall focus on the distribu-tive implications of the Law of Peoples but, before doing so, I need to give an account of Rawls's reasoning in support of its international principles.

The Law of Peoples formulates the fundamental requirements that should govern the foreign policies of liberal democratic states. For Rawls, the fundamental problem of international political theory is to find norms regulating international affairs mutually acceptable for societies with differing institutions and political cultures. He regards cultural and political pluralism among societies as a permanent char-acteristic of the circumstances of international politics, just as pluralism among individuals is a fact of life in free societies. Not all societies conform to liberal standards of social justice but Rawls thinks it is conceivable that there could be non-liberal societies that meet certain moral standards making them acceptable for liberal societies as 'equal participating members in good standing of the Society of Peoples' (Rawls 1999b: 59). This is because of the central place Rawls accords to the idea of toleration and to the requirement of international stability in his theory of international affairs. Toleration, Rawls argues, requires that liberal societies do not impose their values on those non-liberal societies that meet a moral threshold. Principles regulating interna-tional affairs must enable the peaceful coexistence of liberal and decent non-liberal societies in the circumstances of international pluralism.

Rawls's solution to this problem is the Law of Peoples that should regulate the conduct of foreign policy by liberal societies. It consists of eight principles.

1. Peoples are free and independent, and their freedom and independ-ence are to be respected by other peoples.

2. Peoples are to observe treaties and undertakings.
3. Peoples are equal and are parties to the agreements that bind them.
4. Peoples are to observe a duty of non-intervention.
5. Peoples have the right of self-defence but no right to instigate war for reasons other than self-defence.
6. Peoples are to honour human rights.
7. Peoples are to observe certain specified restrictions in the conduct of war.
8. Peoples have a duty to assist other peoples living under unfavourable conditions that prevent their having a just or decent political and social regime (Rawls 1999b: 37).

The principles of the Law of Peoples look very different from the two principles of justice that govern domestic institutions. To understand how Rawls arrives at these principles, we should briefly describe Rawls's terminology and method in *The Law of Peoples*.

Rawls distinguishes between five different kinds of political regimes for the aims of justifying the principles of the Law of Peoples. First, liberal societies have an institutional regime that respects certain basic rights and liberties equally for all their citizens; they give priority to the protection of these rights and liberties over other values; and they provide some measure of redistribution so that citizens can make productive use of these freedoms (Rawls 1999b: 14–15, 23–5). A second category of societies is that of 'decent peoples'. They are not aggressive in their foreign policy and respect the freedom and independence of other societies. They also endorse some human rights though not all the rights included in international human rights documents; they treat their subjects as bearers of rights and obligations; and finally their officials interpret the law as representing a 'common good idea of justice' (Rawls 1999b: 63–78). Third, 'outlaw states' include societies which are aggressive towards other societies and tend to violate human rights (Rawls 1999b: 80–1, 90). Fourth, there are societies burdened by unfavourable conditions which are prevented from becoming liberal or decent by their lack of certain economic or cultural resources (Rawls 1999b: 105–13). Finally, 'benevolent absolutisms' honour some basic human rights but, unlike decent societies, their political institutions do not contain procedures for consulting their subjects when making political decisions (Rawls 1999b: 63).

For a world containing such diverse societies, fair principles for regulating international affairs are those that liberal as well as decent societies – 'well-ordered societies', as Rawls together refers to these regimes – can accept. The principles regulate the conduct of foreign policy by liberal peoples. Rawls first outlines foreign-policy principles for liberal states for a scenario where all states comply with these principles and circumstances are favourable for the domestic justice of societies – what Rawls refers to as ideal theory. After this, he considers the implications of the theory for non-ideal theory where one or both of these conditions fail to obtain.

Rawls develops the argument for his eight principles by yet again relying on the construct of an original position. The original position in the international case, however, looks very different from the one Rawls relies on for deriving his principles for domestic justice. First of all, the international original position features representatives of peoples, not individuals. Second, the international original position represents the interests of liberal and decent peoples but other societies are not represented. Membership in the international original position is selective, unlike in the domestic case where all members of society are equally represented (Pogge 2001b: 246). Finally, the criterion of fairness for the Law of Peoples is that it should be acceptable from the points of view of liberal and decent societies. The motivations of parties in the original position, however, are different from those in the domestic case. The goods that parties, that is, peoples, are fundamentally interested in obtaining are not primary goods but the protection of their political independence, their security, territory, and the good of their citizens. Furthermore, they are not motivated to obtain as much of these as possible, only a sufficient measure (Rawls 1999b: 34, 69). Rawls justifies the acceptability of his Law of Peoples by arguing that liberal and decent societies would both find it reasonable and rational to endorse the same principles as a basis of their foreign policy behind a veil of ignorance (Rawls 1999b: 30–5). Rawls defends his approach by arguing that it shows respect to decent non-liberal societies. Respect requires that liberal societies exercise tolerance in their dealings with societies that are not themselves liberal but meet some minimal moral criteria. To impose on them liberal values would be wrong. He regards egalitarian cosmopolitanism illegitimate for this reason (Rawls 1999b: 82–3, 119–20).

4.2.2 *International distributive requirements*

How does the Law of Peoples bear on international distributive requirements? The main negative thesis of *The Law of Peoples* is that there are no
egalitarian principles of distributive justice applying at the international
level (Rawls 1999b: 115–20). It acknowledges international distributive
obligations but holds that principles regulating such obligations are
not the same as, not even continuous with, those liberal egalitarian
principles of justice Rawls defends in the domestic case. International
distributive obligations have three important characteristics. First, they
hold between states and not between individuals. Second, they are not
egalitarian in the sense that they do not demand an ongoing process
of distribution reducing socio-economic inequalities across nations or
among individuals globally. They specify a threshold level of assistance
above which international aid is no longer a requirement. Finally, our
distributive obligations to outsiders are conceived of as duties of assistance, better described as a humanitarian concern rather than demands
of justice.

What explains the difference between international and domestic
distributive requirements? As Rawls sees it, there is a division of moral
labour between domestic and international societies: the well-being of
individuals is primarily the responsibility of their own societies while
the international community is required to create and uphold conditions among which well-ordered domestic societies can operate (Beitz
1999b: 518). International principles consider the interests of states or
politically organised peoples, not individuals.

This understanding of the justification of international principles
stands in contrast with how Rawls justifies domestic principles of
justice. In the domestic case, the well-being of individuals is foundational in choosing principles for just institutions. When institutions are
unjust, they are condemnable because of their effects on the well-being
of those individuals to whom injustice is done. In *The Law of Peoples*,
by contrast, Rawls's ultimate concern in justifying international principles is that internally just or decent societies can flourish. Individual
well-being has no direct role in the justification of principles for
international affairs: its significance is at best derivative. So long as the
political institutions of societies are just or at least decent, and a set of
principles for international conduct maintains conditions under which
such domestic institutions can flourish, there is no further question

about how domestic or supranational institutions affect individuals (Rawls 1999b: 119–20). The justifications of domestic and international principles are discontinuous.

Owing to this moral division of labour between states and the international community, international distributive requirements to which the Law of Peoples gives rise are far less demanding than principles of justice for domestic societies. Any substantial distributive obligation across countries would be either unnecessary or undesirable. Nonetheless, the Law of Peoples gives rise to some limited international distributive requirements. It prescribes a duty of assistance that liberal states owe to societies burdened by unfavourable economic and cultural circumstances, and it also requires the maintenance of certain standards for fairness in trade 'to keep the market free and competitive' (Rawls 1999b: 43).

The duty of assistance differs significantly from egalitarian requirements of justice that Rawls defends in the domestic case. A prominent difference between the duty of assistance and domestic requirements of justice is that the former ceases to apply once a distributive threshold is met whereas the latter requires ongoing egalitarian transfers. The Law of Peoples requires that liberal states provide some assistance to countries that are prevented from developing liberal or decent institutions by their lack of certain economic or cultural resources. Once these countries have the means for securing human rights for their subjects and for upholding well-ordered institutions, however, international distributive requirements no longer hold. The Law of Peoples does not contain egalitarian requirements of distributive justice that regulate economic inequalities among societies in an ongoing manner (Rawls 1999b: 106). In Rawls's words, the practical difference between the duty of assistance and obligations of distributive justice applying in the national domain is that the former has a 'target and a cutoff point' (Rawls 1999b: 119). The world's poor are to be assisted up to a point where their societies are just or decent. At this point citizens' right to subsistence is secured by their governments. No egalitarian distributive requirements obtain across counties beyond this point. International distributive requirements leave room for large and constantly increasing international inequality (Pogge 2001b: 251).

Furthermore, because it is concerned with the international conditions necessary to enable just or decent political institutions within societies, the Law of Peoples does not impose any direct constraint on domestic or international distribution among individuals. Indirectly it does require the satisfaction of some material minimum in well-ordered societies because, by definition, they satisfy a number of basic human rights including the right to subsistence. Its concern for distribution among individuals is limited in two ways, however. First, the primary responsibility for securing a material minimum for individuals rests with national political societies. The duty of assistance by other states is activated only if the national political society in question cannot secure some basic human right. Second, the content of distributive require-ments which the Law of Peoples justifies is much more limited than what Rawlsian principles of justice demand. Once subsistence rights are secured, there is no further question about the extent of domestic and international inequalities. Because the satisfaction of basic human rights requires far less than the fair equality of opportunity and the difference principles do, international principles allow for inequalities among individuals both within and across state borders well beyond those that Rawls's theory of justice tolerates in the domestic case (Beitz 2000: 688).

Why does *The Law of Peoples* restrict the scope of egalitarian justice to the domestic domain? Rawls regards the institutions of nation-states as necessary to generate relatively demanding distributive requirements for a number of reasons. In the following sections I shall consider four arguments implicit in *The Law of Peoples*: these regard domestic institu-tions as necessary for the existence of egalitarian requirements insofar as they:

1. are the causes of the wealth or poverty of nations;
2. represent mechanisms through which members of nations acquire collective responsibility for their governments' policies;
3. are necessary for the preservation of natural resources;
4. make distributive equality a moral demand by connecting it with other values.

4.2.3 Domestic causes of the wealth of nations

The first argument regards domestic political and economic institutions as central for generating requirements of egalitarian justice because they cause the people subject to their rule to be wealthy or poor. They have a major role in bringing about the prosperity or poverty of nations.

Rawls thus rejects demands by cosmopolitans who have called for more egalitarian international redistribution than *The Law of Peoples* allows for.[4] Ongoing distributive transfers to outsiders are unnecessary, and cosmopolitan requirements of international distributive justice cannot be justified by the same considerations that make the basic structure the appropriate domain for distributive justice at the domestic level.

Rawls provides the following empirical argument to motivate the moral division of labour between international principles and domestic justice. Assuming that natural resource endowment plays no significant role in determining the quality of domestic institutions, Rawls argues that the primary determinants of a society's level of well-being are internal to the society. A set of background economic institutions fostering innovation and investment, stable political institutions, and a public culture that is conducive to economic growth, are likely to result in a higher average level of well-being in a society than that which a different set of economic and political institutions and a culture less conducive to economic development would engender.[5] Variation in per capita levels of natural resources among countries is only marginally important for explaining their citizens' well-being. Given that the crucial factors in the country's well-being are internal to the country's institutions, there is no need for the application of more robust principles of international justice than the duty of assistance (Rawls 1999b: 117). It is sufficient for international principles to make sure that each society can become and remain just or decent.

This argument has invited criticism on empirical grounds. Its opponents challenge the claim that the sources of global poverty are primarily domestic.[6] Granting that natural resource endowment is not the main determinant of economic output, it does not follow that domestic factors are decisive. Natural resource endowment and domestic social and political institutions and culture are not the only factors determining how a country fares. The global institutional system and the policies of other countries have a significant impact on domestic welfare. This means that the empirical question about the primary reasons for a country's wealth is not settled. It is doubtful whether domestic political and economic culture and institutions are so powerful as to override these external influences on a country's well-being.

Furthermore, the argument from the domestic origin of differences in economic growth presupposes that there is a clear-cut distinction between domestic and other determinants of a society's wealth, and it is the domestic causes that carry the day. As Thomas Pogge has force-fully argued, however, in the global division of labour, domestic and external causes are not independent. External factors may significantly determine both what domestic factors come about and also what effects they have. First, it may be the case that domestic economic and politi-cal institutions have a specific effect on a country's development only because a given set of international factors operate. With a different set of international institutions the effect of domestic institutions would be different. Second, what domestic culture and institutions develop in a given society may also be significantly influenced by external factors. Let's see three examples for the impact of international institutions and the policies of other nations on domestic welfare. Pogge has stressed the impact of the global institutional scheme. He emphasises that domestic policies in developing countries are frequently shaped by corrupt, incompetent and often undemocratic elites rather than by the citizenry. Furthermore, Pogge forcefully argues that the current global institutional order contributes to this phenomenon by encouraging conduct by the elites that is not in the interests of their constituents. For example, international law grants the right to recognised governments to sell their nation's natural resources. Because this right is independ-ent of how the rulers acquired their power, it provides a strong incen-tive to military leaders in resource-rich developing countries to try to seize power by coup and rule the country without answering to the citizenry. Successful coup leaders can protect their power by repressing their subjects with arms purchased from resource revenues, with help from their generously funded peers in the military. The end result is bloody civil wars and undemocratic governance leaving the poorest in destitution. Another example concerns international borrowing. Rulers are entitled under international law to borrow funds from abroad in the name of their country. They often do so and thereby impose interna-tionally binding legal obligations on the whole of the citizenry without democratic legitimation. These funds help the rulers to stay in power in the face of popular opposition. Instead of development, the funds are used for strengthening the military loyal to the ruler and for oppressing the population. Loans taken out by toppled dictators while in power also compromise the capacity of the newly elected democratic gov-ernment to implement structural reforms that could benefit the poor in the long run (Pogge 2002: 118–22). The examples of international resource and borrowing privileges illustrate how international institutions and practices shape domestic policies in developing countries and thereby perpetuate poverty and social instability. Furthermore, it is not only international institutions that can have a negative influence on domestic policies in developing countries and contribute to injustice but also the policies of other countries. As we saw in Chapter 3, health and education policies in affluent countries have a significant impact on health outcomes in developing countries insofar as they contribute to the international brain drain of health personnel. Therefore, even if domestic factors indeed significantly influence a country's status in world economy, it is not at all true that external factors are not at least as important. These factors may determine society's capacity to develop and the direction of its development through shaping domestic political and economic culture and institutions. If external factors significantly influence a country's well-being either directly or indirectly, Rawls's claim, that there is no case for international principles of distributive justice, is not justified. Surely, there may be no clear distinction between the effects of domestic and external factors, and therefore serious epistemic difficulties can arise when we want to distinguish between various factors and evaluate their impacts on growth. This is an empirical issue, however, which requires careful assessment on the basis of social scientific data. Rawls fails to provide arguments for his position, hence his restriction of international distributive requirements to a duty of assistance is not supported by his empirical thesis.[7]

To see the real force of the argument, however, let us bracket the debated empirical issue about whether domestic or international factors are the most important determinants of domestic welfare and concentrate, instead, on a related normative point that can support Rawls's position.

4.2.4 *National responsibility and the unfairness of international redistribution*

Rawls's next argument, developed in more detail by David Miller, highlights a normative consideration that can support restricting demands for redistribution to domestic societies. Rawls and Miller argue that members of nations are collectively responsible for the development or backwardness of their own society (Rawls 1999b: 117–18; Miller 1999: 194; Miller 2007). How a country fares, they argue, largely depends on the choices made by the citizenry. What set of freedoms, opportunities, and goods is available to members of a society is determined by the political decisions they have collectively taken. If international principles require redistribution from wealthier to poorer countries, they unfairly penalise societies that have been prudent in the conduct of their economic and political affairs, and unfairly benefit societies that have not. Domestic political and economic institutions are important, then, because they provide mechanisms through which members of political communities acquire shared responsibility for their economic well-being.

To illustrate the contrast between the Law of Peoples and cosmopolitan requirements demanding international redistribution on grounds of justice, Rawls proposes a thought experiment. Imagine two societies with identical initial conditions: suppose they have the same level of gross domestic product (GDP) and the same size of population, making their GDP per capita equal. Society A decides to industrialise while B prefers the leisurely life so it does not industrialise. In A, as a consequence, in the course of several decades both productivity and the per capita domestic product have increased while those of B remained constant. Rawls thinks that, under these circumstances, cosmopolitans would require redistribution from A to B because standards of living in A now exceed living standards in B and inequality is increasing. Rawls argues that redistributing from A to B under these circumstances would be unfair because it would require members of A to undertake some burden that would not have been necessary had B conducted its affairs more prudently. They would end up subsidising the expensive leisurely lifestyle of people in B. The same argument would apply in the case of population policy: a country that now has a lower per capita domestic product because it has failed to carry out an effective policy of controlling population growth does not have a fair claim to resources against a country that is richer because it has effectively controlled its population. Because in both cases members of a society have made sacrifices that members of the other did not – consumed fewer resources, raised fewer children – it would be unfair to require the former to make up for the imprudent choices of the latter. Therefore, Rawls concludes, considerations of national responsibility preclude the existence of robust and globally valid requirements of distributive justice.

Is this argument against international principles of distributive justice sound? I believe it is not. Notice that the argument makes two crucial assumptions. First, it assumes that it is unfair to reduce or eliminate distributive differences between agents that result from choices for which the agents are responsible. Second, it assumes that societies have political features by virtue of which their members can be treated as agents responsible for the decisions of their governments and liable for their results. I will now examine both of these assumptions in detail.

Let's start with the first assumption. Is it convincing to argue that it is unfair to reduce or eliminate inequalities that are due to choices for which the agents are responsible? This would be plausible only against a just background. Arguably, however, the international domain does not meet this requirement: the background against which nations make their choices is not just. Thus, Rawls's conclusion that there are no substantial global distributive requirements does not follow. Let me explain. The force of the argument from national responsibility derives from its supposed analogy with individual responsibility. The most plausible way individual responsibility could be made relevant for justifying distributive obligations is to place the argument in the framework of a recently prominent version of egalitarian liberalism. Many contemporary egalitarians advocate a position that has been called luck egalitarianism in the literature. Luck egalitarians subscribe to the view that distributive differences among individuals should reflect only the choices of individuals themselves and should not reflect their social circumstances or natural endowments. It is unfair for one person to be worse off than another through no fault of his/her own. According to this doctrine, the task of distributive justice is to correct for disadvantages that individuals have owing to factors beyond their control. On the other hand, it also follows from luck egalitarianism that individuals should be held responsible for their circumstances if these result from their voluntary choices, however imprudent or unwise they may have been. Therefore, if Jones is worse off than Smith because he/she prefers surfing to working hard, society should not compensate him/her for his/her relative disadvantage.[8] Society's responsibility is to maintain just background conditions in which individuals can freely decide how to conduct their lives, and individuals should live with the results of their voluntary choices.[9]

Rawls's and Miller's national responsibility argument adapts the luck egalitarian position to distribution across societies. A closer look at the role of responsibility in luck egalitarianism, however, reveals that, from taking nations to be agents that should be held responsible for their choices, it does not follow that no international distributive requirements are justified. The reason is that there are two considerations at work in luck egalitarianism: those of individual responsibility and background equality.[10] Agents are expected to bear the costs of their choices only if these choices are made against the background of fair initial conditions. All disadvantages for which agents are not responsible should be eliminated to provide for equal starting positions. Assuming nations are agents that can be held responsible, they can be required to bear the costs of their choices only against a background of global equality. Therefore, someone who wants to defend the argument from national responsibility on a luck egalitarian basis has to require at the same time the maintenance of initial equality among nations. International principles should be such that they maintain appropriate background conditions against which political societies can autonomously decide how they conduct their internal affairs. Luck egalitarianism would justify redistribution between nations.

In particular, the maintenance of background justice across nations requires international redistribution on two grounds. First, societies must be compensated for the unequal global distribution of natural resources before they can be held responsible for their collective decisions.[11] Second, besides equalising natural resource endowments, background justice requires eliminating further disadvantages for which nations are not responsible, such as disadvantages arising from external economic, social or political factors strongly affecting domestic institutions and policies. We discussed in the previous section that domestic factors, such as beliefs and values in a society, may not be the most important, let alone the only, determinants of domestic policy decisions and their outcomes. Characteristics of a country's involvement in the world political economy and in international institutions can be just as important, if not more important. As Thomas Pogge has stressed, external factors can be part of the explanation of both why people in A and B made their respective decisions in the way they did and also why these decisions have a specific impact on their standards of living. The global institutional scheme including the resource and borrowing privileges, as well as the policies of other nations, significantly influence how a country fares. Mechanisms through which external forces contribute to poverty undermine the national responsibility argument against cross-country obligations of justice. Even if we regard it unfair to reduce or eliminate inequalities between agents that are due to choices for which the agents are responsible, it does not follow that redistribution across nations is unfair. Nations may not be responsible for these inequalities insofar as they result from unequal starting positions in natural resource endowment and from the impact of international institutions and foreign governments.

So far, we have assumed that nations are agents that can be held responsible for their choices. Nations are composed of individuals who make their own choices, however. This makes it necessary to examine now the assumption that members of societies can be treated as agents responsible for the decisions of their governments and liable for their outcome. Cosmopolitan critics of Rawls have argued that individuals rarely can be held responsible for their society's relative economic standing and that this calls for egalitarian international distributive obligations. I shall discuss three cases that are particularly problematic for the concept of collective national responsibility for cross-country inequalities: non-democratic societies, dissenting minorities in democracies, and future generations.[12]

In the case of non-democratic states, policy decisions may have been made by those in power without the participation of citizenry, hence without reflecting their informed preferences. This might well be the case in what Rawls refers to as decent hierarchical societies where subjects are consulted about political decisions but, at least for some groups, 'their views may be systematically and routinely ignored' (Caney 2002: 116). For instance, as Simon Caney argues, a decent society is compatible with denying some of their subjects' democratic voting rights either by lacking democratic institutions altogether or by restricting their democratic institutions only to a privileged class or race in society (Caney 2002: 101). Citizens lack effective means to shape their government's policies. In the case of non-democratic societies, the plight of the poor is arguably not a result of their own individual choices but due to factors beyond their control; thus, they should not be held responsible for their poverty. It follows, then, that affluent foreign societies are required by justice to eliminate their unfair advantage over the oppressed poor. The disadvantages of the latter are not a result of their own choices.

Consider next democratic nations. Even in a properly functioning liberal democracy, there are people who disagree with, or voted against, the policy that has been democratically chosen. Suppose a sizeable minority voted against the majority position which, in turn, results in disadvantages that afflict the society as compared to other nations

that follow different policies. It would be unreasonable to hold these
dissenters responsible for the results of these democratic decisions by
any conception of responsibility that links responsibility with individual
action. Let me explain. Luck egalitarianism holds that no one should
be worse off than others due to reasons beyond his/her own control.
When dissenters vote against government policy that is detrimental
to society and end up losing, their votes in no way contribute to the
disadvantage suffered by themselves and their fellow citizens. They are
worse off than their counterparts in other countries through no fault of
their own and, according to luck egalitarians, are owed compensation
for their disadvantage. Furthermore, even for those who have voted in
support of government, it would be problematic to regard the country's
laws and policies as the outcome of their own decision because, under
the conditions of modern democratic politics, individual votes usually
do not make any difference to the outcome (Dworkin 1996: 28). If an
individual has no impact on political decisions, by the standard of individual responsibility we accept in everyday life, he/she cannot be held
responsible for the distributive outcomes they generate which is also
central to luck egalitarianism (Dworkin 1986: 172).[13]

A defender of national responsibility might argue that dissenters
are responsible for imprudent policies they have opposed. Focusing
on voting as a criterion for responsibility is focusing on the wrong
choice. Even dissenters contribute in various ways to bringing about
government policies they reject. For example, by sharing attitudes and
beliefs with the majority, they may nurture a political culture where
imprudent decisions can take place.[14] By being members of the political
community, they are implicated in the choices they have opposed. For
this reason, the relevant choice for determining collective responsibility
is the decision whether to emigrate. Insofar as citizens had a choice to
leave their country and have decided to stay, they are responsible for
its policies and should be held liable for their outcomes. This objection fails, however. Because emigration is prohibitively expensive for
most people, it is unreasonable to hold those who have decided to stay
responsible for government policies on account of this choice (Segall
2010: 161).

Finally, according to the luck egalitarian position future generations
cannot be held liable for the imprudent choices of their predecessors. The reason is the same as the one at work in the cases of non-
democratic states and contemporary dissidents: luck egalitarianism

holds that people should not be adversely affected by factors beyond their control. Decisions about economic or population policy made by others before someone was born are clearly beyond that someone's control. Therefore, it would be unfair to require members of future generations to bear the burdens of the choices of past generations within the same nation. As we saw earlier, individuals can be expected to bear the costs of their choices only if these choices are made against the background of fair initial conditions, that is, an initial equality is secured by social institutions. This requirement calls for institutions maintaining background equality on the global level. One function of these background institutions is to make sure that individual agents start out with equal opportunities and are not unfairly burdened by inequality resulting from the past choices of their forebears.

Maintaining background justice across generations requires periodic global transfers for two reasons. Individuals must be compensated for the unequal global per capita distribution of natural resources. Because population growth affects per capita resource levels, differences in population policies across countries must be accounted for. Furthermore the adverse effects of economic decisions by past generations must be countered. Because future generations are not responsible for the prosperity or poverty of their nation insofar as it is based on the choices of their predecessors, global redistribution is required to give individuals an equal chance to obtain prosperity. Consider an analogy with two families. Suppose two families start out with equal resources but end up hugely unequal in fifty years' time as a result of their respective choices. Members of one family have been hard working and have made wise investments which have made them much richer than members of the other family who have adopted a leisurely lifestyle. When deriving principles for domestic justice, Rawls does not conclude in *A Theory of Justice* that the rich family is exempt from taxation on account of the prudent choices they made. On the contrary, he argues that one of the main tasks of the basic structure is to correct for the distributive differences across families in order to provide equal opportunity for everyone. Analogously, global equality of opportunity must be secured in the background before individuals can be required to bear the costs of their own choices.

In the face of these familiar problems with holding individuals responsible for their nations' imprudent choices, David Miller objects that, although dissenters and future generations are not morally responsible for choices made by others democratically, they are liable for the costs resulting from their country's policies for reasons of fairness. Because those who find themselves in a minority in the case of a particular decision may be on the winning side in other cases, so the argument runs, they are required by fairness to share the costs when these decisions turn out to bring with them disadvantages (Miller 2007: 119–20). This argument relies on a conception of fairness according to which participants in an ongoing cooperative practice who derive benefits from it are required to contribute their fair share to maintaining it. Those who fail to contribute are free-riding on the effort of others and are for this reason unfair to other participants.[15] In reply to Miller's argument, there are two things to note. First, considerations of fairness may not apply in the case of non-liberal societies which exclude certain sections of their population from political decision-making. These groups probably end up marginalised and their interests neglected; thus it is implausible to claim that they benefit from the scheme. Second, even if this argument may hold for the decisions of contemporaries in democracies, it certainly cannot justify having to bear the consequences of the choices of previous generations. Considerations of fairness cannot justify such a requirement because we do not have duties of fairness to our predecessors who by assumption cannot benefit from our decisions.

To sum up, the argument from national responsibility cannot establish that there are no globally valid requirements of justice in a way that is compatible with luck egalitarianism. There is no complete overlap between the group of people subject to a state's political institutions and those who suffer relative deprivation as a result of their own choices. It is wrong to describe domestic political and economic institutions as mechanisms through which members of political communities acquire shared responsibility for their well-being. First, the national-responsibility argument is based on the incorrect empirical assumption that global poverty is entirely due to domestic injustices that are largely home-grown, without external pressures explaining them. Third-world poverty, however, is partly caused by undue interference and incentives by international institutions or foreign governments. Second, the argument ignores that societies must be compensated for the unequal global distribution of natural resources before they can be held responsible for their collective decisions. Finally, it assumes that political communities should be treated as agents responsible for their governments' policies and liable for their results. This assumption, however, turned out to be false in the case of non-democratic societies, dissident minorities and future generations. Someone living in a country that is poor because of the decisions of ruling elites, democratic majorities he/she opposed or previous generations cannot plausibly be held liable for bearing the costs of imprudent domestic policies resulting in a much lower stand-ard of living or life expectancy than people in other countries face. In these cases many of those suffering disadvantage are more realistically described as the victims of the choices of others, rather than the authors of those choices themselves (Beitz 2000: 692; Pogge 2001b: 253).

4.2.5 States' responsibility for maintaining resources

A further reason against the applicability of requirements of distributive justice to the global domain regards the political institutions of nation-states as instrumental in protecting natural and social resources. In the context of justifying the territorial rights of states, Rawls argues that an essential function of governments is to 'be the representative and agent of a people as they take responsibility for their territory and its environmental integrity, as well as for the size of their population' (Rawls 1999b: 39). Rawls regards this justification of nation-states as analogous to the justification of the institution of property. In his view, the point of the institution of property is to prevent some asset from deteriorating by assigning a specific agent responsibility for maintain-ing it, and to require that the agent bear the costs of not doing so (Rawls 1999b: 8, 39). Property rights create an incentive for agents to preserve the resource rather than to deplete it. Territorial states, too, in Rawls's view, perform this function; they preserve natural and social resources within their territory for the benefit of future generations. This argument, too, employs the notion of responsibility but in a differ-ent sense than the unfairness argument. This time the claim is not that it is unfair to demand of some people to cover the costs of imprudent choices of others because the latter are responsible for their own depri-vation in the sense of having brought it about. The current argument is forward-looking as it is concerned with the value of preserving natural and social resources.

Rawls's argument can be spelled out as follows. Natural and social resources within a territory should be preserved to a reasonable extent so that future generations be given a fair opportunity to be governed by well-ordered institutions and to achieve prosperity. The preservation of natural and social resources requires the pursuit of prudent social and economic policies: for example, population growth should be controlled and investment and savings rates should be kept at an appropriate level. Theoretically, this consideration is compatible with a wide range of institutional schemes. Rawls argues, however, that the system it justifies is a system of states, that is, a system consisting of territorially based, decentralised political units with exclusive jurisdiction over their territories. Though Rawls does not discuss the benefits of territorial governance, the argument can be made that territorial institutions capable of issuing and enforcing authoritative commands can resolve collective-action problems characterising the exploitation and provision of crucial resources.[16] This leaves us with two available alternative schemes: a world state, exercising territorial jurisdiction over the whole planet, and a system of nation-states with territorial rights over portions of the Earth's territory. Rawls favours the system of nation-states for the following reason.[17] He argues that a world government, vested with the powers to make and enforce authoritative decisions worldwide, would not be desirable because it would result in either global despotism or constant fight between subgroups whose members are tied together by strong affinity due to sharing a common culture. For political institutions to motivate support for themselves, they must rely on shared feelings of loyalty and fellow feeling among those they purport to govern. These features, Rawls assumes, are possessed by nations because they are united by 'common sympathies' (Rawls 1999b: 23). A world government, by contrast, would not be able to generate support this way and would be unlikely to carry out its task successfully. It follows that the only viable institutional configuration that can successfully carry out the requirement to preserve resources is the system of nation-states, with each nation taking responsibility for its territory (Rawls 1999b: 36, 48). Does this position rule out the global application of requirements of distributive justice? Depending on the institutional configuration within which it takes place, global redistribution may be unfeasible or undesirable.

First, the global application of distributive justice may be unfeasible if it requires supranational institutions. It is helpful to consider at this point an argument given by David Miller for national self-determination. Miller argues that political institutions can successfully implement principles of justice only if they govern members of a single nation. The reason for this is that systems of justice can be put into practice only if they are supported by mutual trust among their subjects: we are motivated to cooperate and do our fair share in upholding just institutions only if we are assured that others will do their share in turn. Because Miller assumes the required trust exists only among fellow nationals, he argues that it is desirable that each state is made up of members of a single nation. States can do their job successfully only if they govern a relatively homogeneous group of people who see themselves as sharing ties of solidarity with one another (Miller 1995: 90–8). An implication of Miller's argument is that supra-state institutions, comprising several national groups, are not viable. If the global application of principles of justice presupposes global institutions, global distributive requirements cannot be implemented.

Second, international egalitarian distributive requirements would be undesirable if they involve transfers between nation-states. Assuming we need nation-states to preserve and supply natural and social resources, one might argue that governments would not have an incentive efficiently to perform this function within their jurisdiction if substantial international transfers were required. Demanding redistribution may create perverse incentives for governments to behave irresponsibly, that is, to pursue policies that result in a lower level of average well-being because they could expect to be bailed out by other societies. For example, a country may decide to keep its savings and investment rate low and consume a large part of its product instead, or not to control population growth, and expect aid from other countries that fare better as a result of their policies. In such a case, there are reasons against direct redistribution between countries besides the alleged unfairness of these transfers.

The argument from states' responsibility to maintain resources is ultimately unpersuasive. Consider two reasons why the global application of principles of justice is not defeated even if they require substantial global distributive transfers. First, one can challenge the point that the only two feasible alternative institutional schemes are a world state, with powers analogous to nation-states, and the system of nation-states in its current form. Within available alternative schemes the global application of distributive justice is not unfeasible. Rawls's argument assumes territorial states in their current form with sovereign governments in charge of making and enforcing distributive decisions within a demarcated territory. Political authority need not necessarily be located at one level, however. Alternative, multilayered, global institutional configurations may be feasible and superior to these two extremes. One such alternative has been proposed by Thomas Pogge who advocates a multilayered global institutional scheme in which authority is 'vertically dispersed' rather than concentrated at the level of nation-states. Pogge argues that this system would be superior to the system of nation-states because, by dispersing authority over various levels rather than concentrating it in states, it could significantly reduce the likelihood and the intensity of conflicts within and among states, 'thereby reducing the incidence of war, poverty, and oppression' (Pogge 2002: 181–9). Another alternative to nation-states and a unitary world state is a multilayered global institutional system consisting of a mixture of territorially and functionally defined authority. Such a system would disperse authority between substate, state and supra-national levels of territorial institutions as well as institutions with a functionally defined jurisdiction (Kis 2001: 223; Miklós 2009b). If any of these systems of institutions can solve the problem of resource preservation while, at the same time, maintaining international distributive justice, it is superior to the other two alternatives Rawls considers. As long as Rawls has not shown the impossibility of a superior set of institutions, he cannot prove that no principles of international justice apply (Pogge 2002; Pogge 1994; Kuper 2000: 656).

Leaving aside alternative schemes, Rawls's argument is unsuccessful even for territorial governance. Even if we grant that institutions with the powers of territorial states are necessary for preserving and supplying resources, Rawls's and Miller's contention, that supranational institutions would be unable to elicit sufficiently strong adherence from their subjects because they lack the sentiment of fellow nationality, is unfounded. As we saw, Rawls and Miller regard the strong affinity existing among fellow nationals as necessary to generate support for state institutions and carry out the demands of justice, and they argue that this element is missing or significantly weaker at the global level. Many have noted, however, that the circle of affinity is historically variable and, with time, the range of feelings of solidarity may extend to ever larger groups of people (Beitz 2000: 683; Caney 2005: 175).[18] Nation-states themselves could not have developed if this were not so because their institutions were built on very heterogeneous and culturally diverse populations. The history of nation-states itself proves the weakness of the Rawlsian argument. Not only do we learn from this history that motivational capacities are variable but it also convincingly shows that they are influenced by institutions themselves. Thus, even though a theory of global justice needs to take motivational constraints into account when designing institutions, a proposed scheme is not invalidated by showing that it is incompatible with existing motivations. Just global institutions can generate their own support in the long run.

In addition to challenging the argument that egalitarian international transfers would be unfeasible, these points also undermine the claim that such transfers would be undesirable. If there is a feasible alternative global institutional scheme that preserves resources globally while at the same time maintaining international distributive justice, global transfers within this scheme do not undermine the scheme's capacity to preserve resources. The Rawlsian argument can show at best that international transfers are undesirable only if they take place within the current system of nation-states. It cannot show that global distributive requirements within a multilayered global institutional system or within global territorial governance are undesirable.

Finally, showing that global distributive transfers are unfeasible or undesirable is not sufficient to invalidate the global application of principles of justice. As Thomas Pogge has argued, principles of justice provide the criteria by which available alternative institutional schemes are to be comparatively evaluated. They do not prescribe any particular set of institutions in abstraction from available alternatives. Rawlsian principles of justice would require choosing from among feasible alternative schemes the one that best approximates the goal of providing for equal liberties, equality of opportunity and of raising the socio-economic position of the worst off globally (Pogge 2006: 207–8). Thus, even if statists can show that demanding global distributive transfers are unfeasible or undesirable, it does not follow that Rawlsian principles of justice do not apply globally. But, in this case, global distributive requirements would be less demanding than domestic ones.

4.2.6 Fairness and the value of equality

Let's examine a final reason why Rawls denies the existence of egalitarian international obligations of distributive justice beyond the duty to assist poor countries to develop well-ordered institutions and to provide for a threshold of subsistence for the desperately poor. Rawls argues that there are neither reasons rooted in the value of equality nor derivative reasons for demanding an egalitarian distribution in the global domain. There are no reasons for global egalitarianism rooted in the value of the value of equality because an egalitarian distribution is not a value in itself: a more egalitarian distribution is not prima facie better than a less egalitarian one. Rawls argues, however, that there are derivative reasons for favouring an egalitarian distribution in the domestic case but not internationally. Equality is good in the context of domestic political and economic institutions because it contributes to other values but such derivative reasons for equality are absent at the international level. In reply to this position, I will argue that, even if equality is not in itself valuable, Rawls has not shown that the derivative reasons that call for distributive equality domestically fail to apply in the international domain.

Rawls argues that distributive equality is required because of its effect on other values such as fairness (Rawls 1999b: 115; Scanlon 2003: 205). Fairness calls for equality of opportunity in political and economic interaction among citizens; thus, it requires the reduction of domestic socio-economic inequalities. Equality of opportunity imposes egalitarian constraints on social and political competition; large social inequalities are objectionable because they disrupt the fairness of political and social processes. Significant social inequalities among participants in political life are detrimental to the fairness of political processes because they lead to large differences in influence on political decisions. Similarly, fairness in social relations can also be undermined by material inequalities through their negative effects on equality of opportunity; unequal background conditions, such as inequalities in education and excessive differences in family income, can render the competition unfair (Scanlon 2003: 205).

What follows from this about equality in the international domain? Rawls argues that the requirement of fairness applies differently in the international and in the domestic cases. The agents whose relations it regulates as well as its substantive requirements differ. In the domestic case, fairness among individuals is the relevant consideration. Internationally, however, the requirement of fairness arises between states that aim to preserve their independence and to maintain just or decent domestic institutions (Rawls 1999b: 42–4, 115). The content of fairness is also different in the international context. Rawls thinks that, by abiding by some provisions for 'fairness for trade', the international community meets the requirement of fairness because this allows communities to be equally represented in international cooperation. Unlike principles of justice in the domestic case, these provisions for fairness in trade do not demand an ongoing correction of adverse distributive effects of free-market processes because their objective is merely to 'keep the market free and competitive'. Affluent countries should avoid exploiting less developing countries but they are not required to reduce global inequality. Cosmopolitan egalitarian requirements, Rawls suggests, cannot be grounded in the value of fairness (Rawls 1999b: 115–20).

Why does fairness not require egalitarian redistribution internationally? The reason lies in Rawls's construction of the original position for the international domain. Rawls describes the international original position as representing states rather than individuals, and he also stipulates that states' main motive in finding principles for regulating international relations is to secure material conditions necessary for maintaining or developing just domestic institutions and to preserve their own independence. Thus, in their choice of principles for international affairs they are not directly concerned about the well-being of their members.

This rationale is not convincing. First, even if the units of representation in the international original position are states rather than persons, equality of opportunity is a value that applies to the relations between them as well, and it calls for the reduction of international inequalities. Second, Rawls has not ruled out substantive egalitarian requirements that might follow from fairness among individuals worldwide.

Suppose first that parties choosing principles for international affairs represent states, not individuals. Thomas Pogge and others have argued that Rawls's stipulation about parties' motivation in the original position is implausible as states are likely to have at least some interest in increasing the material well-being of their members. They would not be satisfied by being secured a minimum threshold of resources on the basis of which they could sustain their institutions (Pogge 1994: 208–9; Beitz 2000: 693–4). Fairness among states in political and social processes calls for reducing international inequalities and justifies more substantial international distributive responsibilities than Rawls allows for.

Consider first political processes. Fairness among states demands more than merely equal voting rights; economic inequalities among states should be reduced as well. Just like individual liberties in the domestic case, states' political liberties have a fair value only if states' distributive shares are not disproportionate (Pogge 2001b: 251). Take the example of international cooperative organisations like the World Trade Organization (WTO). Equal voting rights among member states are often coupled with huge differences in their bargaining power owing to inequality in resources at their disposal. Poor countries have very little influence on the outcome of meetings and, as a result, the terms of international agreements are often unfavourable to them. As Peter Singer argues, agendas are 'set by informal meetings of the major trading powers', so 'once these powers have reached agreement, the results are presented to the formal meeting, but by then they often are a fait accompli' (Singer 2002: 76).

For similar reasons, the fairness of economic interaction is undermined by excessive differences between states' levels of wealth. Free bargaining among parties with formally equal rights but substantially differing endowment with resources leads to unfairness in social cooperation unless there are background institutions in place that balance out excessive differences. When the terms of international economic cooperation are determined by free bargaining among parties, rich countries can use their greater bargaining power to shape the terms of agreement in their own favour. To protect the vulnerable from the adverse cumulative effects of economic interaction, international background institutions must constrain the terms of cooperation. Procedural fairness in political and social processes demands more by way of international distributive requirements than Rawls admits. A duty of assistance securing a minimum threshold for societies, and standards of fair trade to enable the working of competitive markets, are insufficient to neutralise the unfair cumulative effects of free bargaining among highly unequal parties (Pogge 2001b: 249–51).

Even though fairness among states requires reducing socio-economic inequality to secure equality of opportunity, equality of opportunity among nations is compatible with large levels of inequality and is, in itself, unlikely to support full-blown egalitarian requirements globally similar to those Rawls prescribes for the domestic case. Fairness, however, might require the global application of egalitarian requirements beyond equality of opportunity. A further reason why narrowing the focus of egalitarianism to the domain of national political communities is problematic is that it can violate fairness among individuals, not only fairness among societies. Thomas Scanlon argues that, if members of a group have equal claim to a certain benefit, the procedure for distributing this benefit should reflect this equality (Scanlon 2003: 206).[19] A substantively egalitarian distribution of goods can be then required globally by fairness if we can show that people have equal claims to these.

In what contexts can individuals have equal claims to benefits globally? Let's see two cases when individuals have a prima facie equal claim to benefits that could generate a global requirement for egalitarian distribution. The first case concerns the distribution of benefits jointly produced by individuals participating in a mutually beneficial cooperative enterprise. Scanlon argues that participants in such cooperative practices have equal claims to the benefits produced (Scanlon 2003: 206–7). A substantively egalitarian distribution should then characterise the basic institutions of a society which, according to Rawls, comprise such a mutually beneficial cooperation with profound effects on the lives of participants (Scanlon 2003: 207). Rawls fails to show, however, that no such egalitarian requirements apply beyond the boundaries of nation-states because he does not show that the scope of social and economic cooperation coincide with national boundaries. Furthermore, as I will show in Chapter 5, cosmopolitan Rawlsians argue that cooperation in the required sense indeed exists at the global level.[20] If global cooperation produces benefits and burdens with a significant effect on the life prospects of individuals, fairness requires an egalitarian distribution of benefits and burdens among them. To account for fairness among individual participants in the global cooperation, the international original position then must be modified so that it features representatives of individuals rather than states. As we saw in the domestic case, Rawls argues that the requirement to maintain fairness in society necessitates that interpersonal agreements take place against the background of fair conditions securing an equal measure of rights, liberties, and opportunities, and a fair distribution of resources that precludes large differentials in bargaining power. In the absence of such background conditions the cumulative effects of a series of transactions will be unjust even when they were freely made. If we can show that there exists an international analogue to the system of cooperation Rawls postulates for the domestic case, producing significant benefits and burdens determining the life prospects of individuals globally, global egalitarian requirements are justified.

The second case when individuals have prima facie equal claims to benefits globally concerns the distribution of natural resources. As we shall see in Chapter 6, a case can be made for the claim that every person has an equal claim to the Earth's natural resources. In this case, too, fairness would require that the procedure for distributing resources should be responsive to this equality and call for egalitarian distributive requirements worldwide.

To conclude: considerations of fairness do not confine the scope of egalitarian distributive requirements to domestic political and economic institutions. Fairness calls for the reduction of global inequalities in order to secure equality of opportunity in global political and economic processes and to reflect the equal claims individuals have to the products of institutionally governed global cooperation and to natural resources.

4.3 SUMMARY AND CONCLUSION

It is time to sum up the main points we have covered in this chapter. The chapter began with outlining John Rawls's liberal theory of domestic justice. It then presented Rawls's description and justification of principles for regulating the conduct of international affairs as developed in *The Law of Peoples*. In this work, Rawls argues for a restriction of the scope of egalitarian justice to the domestic domain, resisting demands for more substantial international distributive requirements. His argument regards the political institutions of nation-states as necessary to generate egalitarian requirements. He argues against international egalitarian requirements by claiming that domestic institutions:

1. are the causes of the wealth or poverty of nations;
2. represent mechanisms through which members of nations acquire collective responsibility for their governments' policies;
3. are necessary for the preservation of natural and social resources;
4. make distributive equality a moral demand in order to meet the requirement of fairness.

In response to these claims, I hope to have shown that none of these arguments of Rawls is satisfactory. I have argued that:

1. Rawls fails to provide empirical support for his claim that the causes of poverty are primarily domestic;

2. considerations of collective responsibility cannot vindicate Rawls's position because global inequalities are due to factors for which individuals and states cannot be held responsible;
3. global institutions can carry out the task of preserving resources while at the same time maintaining international distributive justice;
4. fairness calls for equality of opportunity in global institutions and is likely to demand substantively egalitarian distribution of the products of global cooperation and natural resources.

In the next chapter I shall rehearse an argument for extending the scope of distributive justice to the global domain. There I will present a cosmopolitan extension of Rawls's theory of justice to the global realm, inspired by the framework of social justice he develops in *A Theory of Justice* and *Political Liberalism*.

Notes

1 See also Rawls, 2001, p. 10.
2 In what follows, I shall refer to Rawls's book as *The Law of Peoples*, in italics, whereas I shall refer to the international principles it defends as the Law of Peoples.
3 Rawls addressed the problem of international justice very briefly in Section 58 of *A Theory of Justice*. There he claims that the law of nations, i.e. norms regulating international conduct of states, would consist of such principles that representatives of states would affirm under appropriately defined conditions. Rawls argues that parties would agree to some familiar principles of international affairs, such as the principle of self-determination, the requirement of non-intervention, the right of self-defence, the requirement that treaties are to be kept, and certain rules of the conduct of just war (Rawls, 1999a, pp. 331–3). *The Law of Peoples* elaborates on these remarks in more detail.
4 For these cosmopolitan positions see Beitz, 1999a, Part III; Pogge, 1989. I present these theories in more detail in the next chapter.
5 In particular, Rawls argues that the most important factors influencing society's well-being are the public culture and 'the religious, philosophical, and moral traditions' of the society, as well as 'the industriousness and cooperative talents of its members'. In making this argument, he draws heavily on the work of David Landes (Landes, 1998) Arguably, all the factors Rawls emphasises are determined by differences in the institutional background across countries (Rawls, 1999b, p. 108).

 6 For an elaborate discussion of this claim, drawing on a rich pool of empiri-
    cal data, see Pogge, 2002. See also Buchanan, 2003, pp. 209–15.
 7 For an attempt to put flesh on Rawls's position and to solve the
    philosophical problem about global justice by relying on data from devel-
    opment economics see Risse, 2005b, pp. 81–117.
 8 The parable of the grasshopper and the ant pre-dates luck egalitarianism.
    Libertarian theorist Robert Nozick famously made use of this argument in
    his case for the minimal state (Nozick, 1974, p. 170).
 9 For defences of this theory see Arneson, 1989; Dworkin, 2000; Cohen,
    1989. For the contrary position see Anderson, 1999; Scheffler, 2003b;
    Daniels, 2003.
10 Here I follow Ronald Dworkin who distinguishes two ethical principles
    underlying his theory of justice: the principle of equal importance, and the
    principle of special responsibility (Dworkin, 2000, pp. 5–6).
11 For similar argument see Wenar, 2002, p. 58.
12 For these familiar problems, with the national responsibility argument,
    see Beitz, 2000; 1999, pp. 526–7; Moellendorff, 2002, pp. 48–9; Fabre, 2007,
    p. 104; Pogge, 1989, pp. 252–3; Caney, 2002, pp. 116–17; Segall, 2010,
    pp. 160–2.
13 Derek Parfit argues that individual votes do make a difference: when
    considering the rationality of our voting, we have to calculate the expected
    benefit of our vote, i.e., we have to multiply the possible benefit that would
    be brought about by a superior alternative by the probability that my vote
    will tip the balance. If stakes are sufficiently high, it is rational for me to
    vote on consequentialist grounds, and I have to vote in a way that secures
    the greatest expected benefit (Parfit, 1984, pp. 73–5). Even if we accept
    Parfit's consequentialist thesis *ex ante*, however, it does not follow that an
    individual vote is subject to judgement of responsibility *ex post*. I would be
    responsible only if it were true that my vote was actually decisive: i.e., had
    I not voted, or had voted differently, the outcome of the vote would have
    been different. If my vote did not tip the balance, as it usually does not
    in democratic decisions involving a large number of people, I cannot be
    held responsible for the outcome on a plausible conception of individual
    responsibility.
14 Think of liberal whites in the racially segregated South or dissidents in
    Nazi Germany (Miller, 2007).
15 The principle was first suggested by Hart (1955) and was also endorsed
    by Rawls in his early work as the principle underlying political obligation
    (Rawls, 1999c, pp. 117–29). The most elaborate and influential defence
    of the principle with regard to political obligation is provided by Klosko
    (1992).
16 For instance, political institutions can help overcome 'tragedy of the

commons' type situations. For a general description of these see Hardin, 1968.

17 Rawls endorses Immanuel Kant's remarks in *Perpetual Peace*, ruling out a world government (Kant, 1992, p. 113).

18 Interestingly, Rawls is not sceptical about the prospect of growing affinity between peoples. He fails to explain, however, why growing affinity between peoples could not lead to a growing affinity among individuals worldwide (Rawls, 1999b, p. 113).

19 For an illuminating discussion of cases when this condition is satisfied, see Nagel, 2002, pp. 113–33.

20 See the arguments in Beitz 1999, Part III; Pogge, 1989; Kuper, 2000; Caney, 2002; Buchanan, 2003, pp. 209–15; Moellendorf, 2002, pp. 68–101.

Chapter 5

RAWLSIAN JUSTICE GLOBALISED

Disagreeing with Rawls's position in *The Law of Peoples*, some cosmopolitans argue that Rawlsian domestic theory of justice should be extended to the global domain. Rawlsian cosmopolitans emphasise that there exists a global basic structure relevantly similar to the domestic ones, and that the same reasons Rawls argues call for the application of distributive justice in the domestic case require the global application of principles of justice. I start this chapter by describing this cosmopolitan argument. Next, I outline some arguments critics make against the applicability of Rawlsian principles of justice in the global domain. These objections to global distributive justice are based on reasons internal to Rawls's domestic theory of justice, in contrast with Rawls' objections in *The Law of Peoples*. I defend the cosmopolitan interpretation of Rawlsian theory by showing that the objections do not warrant limiting the scope of justice to the domestic level because Rawls's rationale for the application of the principles of justice holds for the global domain. Finally, I evaluate the claim that Rawlsian theory would require the international redistribution of natural resources even in the absence of global cooperation.

5.1 THE GLOBAL EXTENSION OF RAWLSIAN THEORY

I presented in detail Rawls's theory of domestic justice in Chapter 4; thus, there is no need to repeat that account here. I will only briefly recapitulate its key features before considering the global extension of this theory. Rawlsian justice is an instance of the relational view because it sees the scope of distributive justice as limited to those individuals who are fellow participants in a scheme of social cooperation. Justice concerns the fair distribution of benefits and burdens from social cooperation. Although Rawls focuses on social cooperation which is mutually advantageous for those participating in it, many have argued that this narrows unacceptably the scope of justice. Social cooperation need not be beneficial for all its participants for principles of justice to be applicable to it, otherwise principles of justice could not condemn schemes of cooperation that fail to benefit some of their participants (Beitz 1999a: 131; Pogge 1989: 20). For this reason, it is more plausible to argue that, whenever significant advantages or disadvantages are produced through cooperation, they should be subject to assessment by the principles of justice (Beitz 1999a: 131). A necessary feature of social cooperation in Rawls's scheme is that it is regulated by the basic institutions of society, or what Rawls calls the basic structure. The institutions of the basic structure 'distribute fundamental rights and duties and determine the division of advantages from social coopera-tion' (Rawls 1999a: 6). The reason why Rawlsian theory is focused on the basic structure of society is that the basic structure has profound effects on the life prospects of individuals subject to it (Rawls 1999a: 7). The contours of social cooperation regulated by the basic structure are consequential for participants because they fundamentally shape individual opportunities, skills and goals, and give rise to inequalities in life prospects.

Because, in economic and social life, we interact with others against the background of the basic structure, our social and economic rela-tions with others cannot be fair unless the basic structure is just. A just basic structure secures and preserves the long-term fairness of social cooperation by specifying background conditions that maintain equal basic rights, liberties, and opportunities, and provide for a fair distribu-tion of resources among its subjects. It precludes large differentials in bargaining power, and mitigates the effect of inequalities in social and natural resources on social relations.

To determine how to structure the basic institutions of society in a fair manner, Rawls relies on a formal argument to derive principles of justice. He asks us to imagine that we are to choose a contract in an original position. Fair principles of justice are those terms that self-interested parties would accept if they were denied knowledge of their social background, their talents and skills as well as their conceptions of the good. Fairness requires that principles of justice do not take into account these contingencies. Under the circumstances of the original position, parties are unable to choose principles that systematically

advantage their personal interests. Morally contingent or arbitrary differences, such as one's sex, race, the social class of one's parents, and
one's inborn natural endowments, are excluded from the justification
of principles of justice (Rawls 1999a: 62–3). Likewise, our conceptions
of the good play no role in their justification, to prevent us from choosing principles of justice that allow us to exercise rights and freedoms
important to us at the expense of rights and freedoms others value
(Rawls 1999a: 16–17).

   Under these circumstances, parties would choose principles of
justice that maximally benefit the worst off to avoid having to suffer the
consequences of the worst-case scenario. They would choose a set of
institutions that secure an expansive set of rights and arrange material
inequalities in a way that favours the poorest. Two principles of justice
provide the standard of fairness by which the distribution of the benefits and burdens of social cooperation should be measured. According
to the first of these, everyone has an equal right to basic liberties. The
second principle demands that people should enjoy fair equality of
opportunity to obtain valuable positions and offices and requires that
socio-economic inequalities should maximally benefit the worst-off
members of society (Rawls 1999a: 53; Rawls 1999a: 72).

   The question arises: what are the outer limits of Rawlsian justice? In
A Theory of Justice, Rawls pre-empts raising this question by stipulating
that he constructs principles of justice for the basic structure *of a society*
which is a 'closed system isolated from other societies' (Rawls 1999a:
7). Cosmopolitan Rawlsians, however, argue that this stipulation is
not justified and conclude that the scope of Rawlsian justice is global.
Cosmopolitans rely on empirical evidence against Rawls's stipulation.
It is documented by a large and growing body of empirical literature
that there is a dense web of international economic and social interactions, as a consequence of which no society can be self-contained.[1]
People's lives are intermingled through the global movement of goods,
capital and persons. International transactions produce substantial
benefits and costs that spread across the world. Furthermore, these
transactions take place against the background of institutions and practices, often subject to a global regulatory structure.[2] Financial and
monetary institutions, trade agreements, international political and
legal institutions have a tremendous impact on the global distribution
of resources. Notable examples include international financial and
economic regimes, such as the International Monetary Fund, the World

Bank, or the World Trade Organization, which largely determine the terms on which resources are produced and distributed worldwide. As a consequence of these global interactions, benefits and costs are produced that would not exist if the world indeed consisted of self-contained societies.

Emphasising the significance of global interconnectedness, cosmopolitan Rawlsians argue that Rawlsian principles of justice should be applied globally. They make the following argument. Current international social and economic interactions constitute a scheme of social cooperation relevantly similar to the domestic cooperation within which Rawls argues that requirements of distributive justice apply. Therefore, principles of distributive justice apply globally.[3] Since state boundaries do not coincide with the limits of social cooperation, nothing justifies limiting the concern of justice to nation-states. This cosmopolitan argument takes a conditional form: if we accept the Rawlsian theory of justice at the domestic level, then, owing to the relevant similarity of the international institutional scheme, principles of justice must be applied globally.

Let me spell out in detail why cosmopolitans think Rawlsian principles apply globally. We saw earlier that, for Rawls, justice is a property of schemes of social and economic cooperation that generate benefits and burdens for their participants. Principles of justice determine the fair distribution of the resulting benefits and burdens. In particular, Rawls is interested in cooperation which is regulated by the basic institutions of society. The basic structure is the locus of justice because it has profound effects on the life prospects of individuals subject to it; it decisively shapes individuals' lives and it does so from the start (Rawls 1999a: 7). Cosmopolitans defending the global validity of Rawlsian justice argue that global cooperation is regulated by a global basic structure that has the same morally relevant characteristics as domestic ones; there are large global inequalities in starting positions which are profoundly shaped by the existing global institutional framework (Pogge 1989: 247; Beitz 1999a; Barry 1973: 129). One's place of birth greatly affects what opportunities are open for a person throughout his/her life. Furthermore, global inequalities in life prospects are, to a large extent, determined by the global institutional system. Because there is a global institutional order which produces significant benefits and burdens largely determining individual life prospects, the whole of this order – including the system of states – is to be evaluated by the standards of justice. If there are superior institutional alternatives, they are to be preferred to the current system of global institutions.

Given that there is a global institutional framework with a pervasive impact on life prospects worldwide, global interaction should take place against a fair background. We saw that Rawls thinks that interpersonal agreements are morally justified only if they are freely entered into under conditions that are fair (Rawls 1993: 266). The global basic structure must regulate global inequalities to ensure that international interactions among persons and groups are fair. Otherwise, the accumulated result of a large number of international interactions would undermine the fairness of future agreements and transactions. Interpersonal agreements which take place against a set of institutions allowing for substantial inequalities in bargaining power, information, rights, liberties, and opportunities are unfair, no matter whether they involve international or domestic transactions. The fairness of the background conditions defined by the global basic structure must be secured and preserved.

What standard of fairness should be used to evaluate the global institutional order? Cosmopolitan Rawlsians argue that this assessment should take place against the standard of the same two principles that Rawls prescribes for the basic structure of national societies (Beitz 1999a: 151; Pogge 1989: 249–50; Barry 1973: 129). They assume that the content of principles of justice is independent of their scope. The mere fact of enlarging the scope of justice should not lead to different principles than those applying in the domestic case. If our relation to the poor in third-world countries is similar to our relation to the poor in our own country in all morally relevant respects, there is no reason that we should owe more to the latter. So the two principles of justice Rawls defends in the case of domestic justice should be applied globally.

Formally, principles of global justice can be derived with the help of a global original position. Like the one Rawls envisages for domestic justice, the global original position would include parties rationally choosing principles on the basis of their self-interest behind a veil of ignorance. In addition to screening out information about parties' socio-economic position and natural assets, however, the veil of ignorance in the global original position would also block parties' knowledge of their membership in specific national political units. They could not know whether they live in a country which is rich or poor, because the country in which we live is just another contingent fact about us that has no normative significance in justifying principles of justice, just as irrelevant as our intelligence, race or social background are. Given this constraint, parties would choose Rawls's two principles of justice with a global scope. If we are barred from knowing which country we live in, we would accept principles of justice that allow only those socio-economic inequalities that benefit the globally worst off and that provide for fair equality of opportunity globally.

The global principles of justice are concerned with the interests of individuals, not states. In other words, justice requires that global institutions should be arranged such that they benefit the poorest people in the world, not the poorest country. Owing to intra-country inequalities, we have no reason to assume the two groups coincide (Beitz 1999a: 152–3). Accordingly, and contrary to Rawls's stipulation in *The Law of Peoples*, the original position in which we derive global principles of justice should represent the interests of individuals, not states. We can justify this assumption in two steps. We can show, first, that individuals should be represented in the global original position, regardless of whether other entities, such as states, are represented. Second, we can further argue that it is only individuals who should be so represented. For suppose, first, that parties in the global original position represented only states which are only concerned with their domestic justice. They would accept a global order consisting of several internally just states, allowing for large differences in life prospects between individuals living in different countries. International transactions would still be characterised by large inequalities in bargaining power. Such an order, however, would permit unfairness to individuals. It is individuals who ultimately have to bear the burdens and benefits global cooperation produces, and these have a profound impact on their life prospects. Because global interpersonal inequalities result to a large extent from the working of international institutions, they should be governed by principles of justice. If excessive social and economic interpersonal inequalities are unjust by the fair equality of opportunity principle and the difference principle, in the case of domestic societies, by the very same reason they must be unjust internationally. The two principles of justice should evaluate alternative global institutional schemes on the basis of their differential effects on the globally worst individual position. It is the globally worst-off representative person whose position matters for justifying alternative institutional schemes (Pogge 1989: 247-8; Beitz 1999a: 152).

Second, it is only individuals who should be represented in the global original position owing to the methodological individualism of Rawls's theory of justice. The fact that Rawls recognises only individuals as 'self-originating sources of valid claims' precludes weighing the interests of states – taken separately from the interests of individuals they represent – against those of individuals (Rawls 1980: 543). States should not be given independent consideration in a global original position (Pogge 1989: 247; Beitz 1999a: 153).

Hence, there are compelling reasons for being concerned with the interests of individuals when assessing alternative principles for the evaluation of the global institutional structure. Furthermore, as Pogge and Beitz argue, Rawls's theory of justice gives us a reason to decide about the favoured global institutional scheme in one single original position rather than in two separate sessions. A single original position for global and domestic institutions avoids taking for granted one aspect of the current global institutional scheme, the state system. This system represents a particular form of political and economic organisation; it is characterised by states with eminent domain and monopoly of coercion in a demarcated territory, making, interpreting and enforcing law within their borders (Pogge 1989: 257). A separate global original position, already taking for granted the system of states, would fail to take account of the effects of the domestic institutions of one state on individuals living in other countries. It would also fail to compare the effects of the current system of nation-states on individual lives with those of other feasible global institutional set-ups. Given normative individualism, it would be unjustified to grant immunity to the state system from assessment in terms of its effects on individual lives (Pogge 1989: 247–8). If an alternative scheme of institutions turned out better to promote the position of the globally least advantaged representative individual, it would be preferred by a Rawlsian conception of justice.

To conclude: the global original position should represent individuals rather than states, and there is no need for two separate sessions to choose principles for domestic and then for international justice. One single session should incorporate both domains in which parties at once choose principles for the global, as well as domestic, basic structures (Pogge 1989: 247; Beitz 2000: 693). These parties under a veil of ignorance would choose Rawls's two principles of justice as the standard for regulating the global basic structure. Rawlsian justice has a global scope.

5.2 ARGUMENTS AGAINST THE GLOBAL EXTENSION

The cosmopolitan argument for the global application of Rawlsian principles of distributive justice provoked various criticisms, however. In the previous chapter I discussed some arguments given by Rawls himself and others against global distributive justice. I regard these arguments as external to Rawls's own theory of justice because they invoke considerations that are not part of Rawls's argument in *A Theory of Justice*. Let us now turn to some other objections to the global extension of Rawlsian justice which I take to be internal to Rawlsian theory. These objections hold that we owe more by justice to fellow nationals than to foreigners even though we might have obligations of justice to both groups. The objections rely on different interpretations of Rawls's characterisation of the basic structure as part of his theory of justice. A common feature of these arguments against a global Rawlsian distributive justice is that they argue that there are morally relevant differences between international interaction and social cooperation characterising domestic societies. In particular, they deny that an international scheme of cooperation exists in the sense relevant for Rawlsian justice. They do not question the existence of international economic, social, political, and legal relationships but they argue that interaction in the international domain is not sufficient for the application of Rawlsian principles of justice. I shall consider three of these objections. They emphasise different aspects of cooperation as necessary criteria for the existence of requirements of justice. The first objection interprets Rawlsian cooperation as consequential interaction through institutions and argues that international interaction differs in degree from the domestic one owing to its less substantial impact. The second and third objections regard Rawlsian cooperation as either involving mutually beneficial cooperation or authoritative political institutions, which they claim the international domain lacks. These two objections see Rawlsian cooperation as different in kind from international interaction. Social interaction – however significant its impacts are – is not sufficient for the existence of requirements of justice because there are other necessary conditions to be taken into account which are not satisfied for the international domain.

5.2.1 *Insufficient international cooperation*

First, it can be argued that international interconnectedness is insig-
nificant as compared with the domestic one.[4] The greater intensity
of domestic social cooperation can thus be thought to give rise to
stronger domestic distributive requirements than international interaction does. A thought experiment illuminating this objection asks us
to imagine a world of self-sufficient national societies, say with two
autarkic islands.[5] In Rawlsian theory, there would be no requirements
of distributive justice among these societies because there is no social
cooperation between them. Next, suppose that these societies start
to interact with each other marginally, introducing some occasional
exchanges of goods. It seems far-fetched to require that the difference
principle be applied with full force to the world comprising these two
societies. If requirements of justice apply in this scenario, they would at
best concern the distribution of goods that get exchanged between the
two islands. This objection is compatible with cosmopolitanism insofar
as it does not rule out the global application of requirements of justice.
It rules out the global application of Rawls's two principles of justice,
however; international distributive requirements, if they exist, demand
less than domestic ones.

   In reply to this objection, Beitz argues that we can grant that there is
a threshold of interconnectedness above which the difference principle
applies and, at the same time, argue that international interconnectedness is above the threshold (Beitz 1999a: 165–7). As we saw, a crucial
feature of the basic structure that makes it the appropriate subject
of justice according to Rawls is that it comprises a system of institutions that defines individual starting positions and assigns rights and
duties. International cooperation is not analogous to the case of the
two islands because it involves a massive institutional background,
with its institutional rules setting the framework for individual action.
Furthermore, the effect of this institutional scheme on individual well-
being is not marginal, as it was presumed to be in the case of the two
islands.[6] International cooperation is relevantly similar to the domestic
basic structure in that it involves an institutional architecture governing transactions, having a pervasive impact on individual life prospects
(Beitz 1999a: 166; Pogge 1989: 262–3). If the conditions of subjection
to a system of institutions and one's life prospects being significantly
affected by these institutions are jointly sufficient for the application of

Rawls's two principles of justice to these institutions, these principles apply globally.

There is controversy about the actual effects of the global institutional scheme on individual lives. Some theorists argue that this scheme has harmed the poor by making them worse off than they would be without it.[7] The other camp holds that international cooperation has, in fact, made the poor better off, as is shown by an increase in life expectancy and better living standards worldwide than at any other time in human history.[8] This debate can be bracketed for the aims of the current argument, however. No one seriously doubts that there is global cooperation which takes place against the background of a global scheme of institution, with pervasive effects on the lives of most humans. As long as this is the case, the rationale for applying principles of justice to the basic structure also holds in the case of the global scheme of institutions. Significant benefits and burdens are produced in international cooperation, and fairness requires that they ought to be distributed in a just manner (Beitz 1999a: 152).

5.2.2 The lack of mutually beneficial cooperation

The second argument against the global application of the Rawlsian principles also emphasises the disanalogy between domestic cooperation and international interaction, as well as the distributive requirements they generate. Whereas the previous objection argued that there is a difference in degree between domestic and international interaction, the current objection claims that there is a difference in kind between the two domains. Brian Barry argues that the two principles of justice, including the difference principle, come into play only in the context of social cooperation but they cannot be applied globally because the world does not constitute a cooperative scheme in the relevant sense (Barry 1991: 193–5). The mere fact of international interconnectedness, even though it is shaped by various existing international institutions which coordinate the activities of individuals, corporations, and states, does not amount to cooperation in the relevant sense, Barry claims. This argument rules out egalitarian requirements of justice to foreigners though it allows for less demanding distributive obligations to them. What makes egalitarian justice apply in the context of domestic cooperation? According to Barry's interpretation of the Rawlsian theory, justice is based on a requirement of fair play. The duty of fair play requires that participants deriving benefits from an ongoing practice contribute their fair share in maintaining it, on pain of being unfair to other participants (Rawls 1999a: 96).[9] Because Rawls regards society as a scheme of institutions providing benefits to all its members, Barry interprets him to be claiming that the duty of fair play applies to all members of the society. Once there is a scheme of social cooperation providing benefits to its participants, all participants are required by justice to contribute their fair share in maintaining social cooperation. We do not have such duties to foreigners, Barry argues, because there is no international institutional framework from which all of us benefit. International interactions do not constitute cooperation of the relevant kind because the duty of fair play applies in the case of mutually beneficial cooperation only, and international cooperation is not mutually beneficial (Barry 1991: 195). International cooperation is not sufficient to trigger the distributive requirements of Rawlsian justice.

This objection can be interpreted in two different ways. First, Barry might be taken to mean that establishing a just global scheme would not be advantageous to those who are well off *now*. Affluent countries would not find it attractive to institute an international scheme that redistributes much of their resources to the global poor. The reason for this is that the flow of benefits in the foreseeable future would be one way, that is, away from the rich to the poor and, thus, affluent countries would be unlikely to benefit from the scheme. On the whole, they would do better with the current arrangements continued than with a global scheme of institutions satisfying egalitarian principles. So the conditions triggering the duty of fair play do not exist at the international level because it is not true that all parties benefit – or stand to benefit – from switching to a Rawlsian scheme.

This argument against the international applicability of Rawlsian justice rests on a mistaken interpretation of the Rawlsian theory. It compares an existing unjust institutional scheme with a just one and suggests that, for principles of justice to apply to a scheme of cooperation, the transition from the unjust actual scheme to a just one should itself be mutually beneficial. This line of reasoning implies that if advantaged participants under an existing unjust scheme would end up worse off under an available alternative just scheme than they are now, the alternative scheme is not mutually beneficial; thus, by consequence, it is not required by Rawlsian justice. As Thomas Pogge suggests, this is a very unlikely interpretation of Rawls (Pogge 1989: 263–4). It amounts to entrenching any kind of unjust scheme by precluding the application of Rawlsian principles to them because there would always be *someone* who would end up worse off under a just scheme than he/she is under an existing unjust scheme. Slave holders lost some of their advantages in a transition from a slave-holding society to one without slaves, as did men when women's rights gained acceptance (Richards 1982: 277, 289). According to this argument, principles of justice would not apply to any scheme that is not already just, and this is absurd. Rawls does not hold that cooperation in a just scheme should be beneficial to all, including those unjustly advantaged in the current unjust scheme, as compared to their current position.

On the second interpretation, Barry might argue that Rawls's principles of justice do not apply globally because the current global institutional scheme is not mutually advantageous as against the benchmark of non-cooperation. Some people or groups might do better being autarkic and avoid interacting with other people or groups. This argument is very implausible, however. As we saw earlier, cosmopolitan Rawlsians do not regard mutual advantage as a necessary criterion for the existence of requirements of justice. Principles of distributive justice should not be applied only among people who each benefits from co-operating with others. It would be absurd to deny that justice is owed to those who are worse off in an unjust society as a result of interaction with others. Consider the case of slaves before the American civil war: they did not necessarily benefit from the social system of the South; nonetheless it would be impossible to argue that justice was not owed to them. For this reason, cosmopolitan Rawlsians argue that requirements of distributive justice arise among people who interact with one another, following institutions and practices which produce benefits or burdens that would not exist if the social interaction would not take place (Beitz 1999a: 131). The current global institutional system clearly satisfies this condition. Benefits and burdens are produced by social interaction along the lines of the global scheme of institutions, and these benefits and burdens would not exist in the absence of global institutional interaction. Principles of justice should determine the fair distribution of these benefits and burdens.

This argument shows that the mutual benefit criterion should not be used for determining the scope of justice, that is, for identifying the group of persons among whom requirements of justice arise. Interpreted properly, mutual benefit should be a criterion for selecting a distributive scheme from among the multiple available schemes. An institutional scheme generating inequalities among participants can be justified only if we can show that this scheme is beneficial to all participants as compared to the benchmark of complete equality. Note that the relevant comparison is between holdings in the just scheme and a completely egalitarian distribution.[10] Distributive equality is the appropriate benchmark in Rawlsian theory because it reflects the moral equality of persons that is a fundamental element in the theory. Against this benchmark of equality, the difference principle, by construction, embodies a criterion of mutual advantage. A basic structure optimising of the worst-off position across alternative schemes can be presumed to be mutually beneficial for all the participants. Compared to this scheme, a more egalitarian scheme may leave the worst off with a smaller overall share of resources even though their relative share would be higher. The more advantaged are also better off under the scheme favoured by the difference principle than in a scheme with perfectly egalitarian distribution. To conclude, global redistribution would violate the condition of mutual advantage only if such redistribution would leave the global rich worse off than they would be under conditions of distributive equality (Moellendorf 2002: 73). It would be very implausible to claim that this is so.

5.2.3 The lack of political institutions

The third argument, too, denies that there is global cooperation in the relevant sense and concludes that Rawlsian principles of justice do not apply globally. It appeals to the importance of political institutions in delimiting the scope of justice. Mere economic interaction, however widespread and regular, does not constitute a cooperative scheme in the relevant sense, the argument runs, because cooperation in the Rawlsian sense necessarily comprises the political institutions and the legal system of the state as well. What makes the basic structure special for justice is not merely that it exerts profound impact on the lives of individuals from the start; the basic structure, as Rawls understands it, is politically regulated cooperation within which citizens participate, governed by the political constitution and the legal system. The international domain, by contrast, does not contain political institutions similar to those applying domestically. Thus, the argument can be made that there is a qualitative difference between the domestic basic structure with its social and political institutions constituting a special form of cooperation on the one hand, and international economic interaction on the other hand.[11]

We can spell out this argument as follows. Recall that Rawls defines the basic structure as 'the way major social institutions distribute fundamental rights and duties and determine the division of advantages from social cooperation'. The social institutions of the basic structure include 'the political constitution and the principal economic and social arrangements' (Rawls 1999a: 6). These institutions comprise procedural rules determining how laws are enacted, and also substantive norms maintaining background justice and setting the economic framework within which individuals and associations interact. In particular, the basic structure includes the legal norms of property law, contract law and commercial law, all of which circumscribe the production, ownership, exchange and use of resources. It also includes the tax system, with income, property and inheritance taxation setting limits on the ownership of property. These procedural and substantive rules are determined by territorially defined states; relying on their political authority, states make, interpret and enforce rules which apply to all those within a state's territory. Hence, political cooperation, which takes place within territorial states with parameters set by the political constitution and the legal system, is an integral part of social cooperation within the basic structure. Political institutions exercising authority over their subjects and determining the framework of their economic interaction are necessary for the application of Rawlsian principles of distributive justice; thus they circumscribe the scope of egalitarian requirements.

Arguably, no such system exists at the global level because there is no world state with its system of law and property. Hence, Samuel Freeman argues that there is no global social cooperation in the relevant sense that could justify the global application of Rawlsian principles of justice. He claims that there is no global political authority that would determine the economic and distributive framework worldwide independently from the political authority of nation-states; ultimate political authority lies with sovereign nation-states. International trade is largely conducted pursuant to the property and contract laws of one or another country or international treaties resulting from intergovernmental bargaining and diplomacy; it is these laws that regulate economic transactions and settle disputes about rights. Global institutions

have political power only insofar as independent states have granted
them power in accordance with their own constitutions. Furthermore,
the power of global institutions is limited by the capacity of nation-
states to withdraw at any time power they transferred to them.
Therefore, both the empirical claim made by Rawlsian cosmopolitans,
and the normative conclusion they draw from it, are false; there is no
global basic structure in the relevant sense and, consequently, the
scope of Rawlsian justice is not global (Freeman 2006a).

    We can interpret this objection in two different ways because political
institutions can be necessary for justice in two different senses: justice
might presuppose existing political institutions; or political institutions
may be necessary for the implementation of principles of justice.[12]
Consider first the claim that egalitarian justice presupposes existing
political institutions. This would mean that, in the absence of political
institutions governing a group of persons, no requirements of egalitarian justice would exist among these persons. Because there are no
global political institutions exercising authority over their subjects and
setting the economic framework for their interaction, there are no
requirements of egalitarian justice with a global scope. This objection
to the global application of Rawlsian justice has limited force, however,
and it is ultimately unsuccessful. First, it is important to note that this
objection would not necessarily preclude requirements of distributive
justice with a global scope for reasons I have mentioned in reply to the
political conception of justice. One can argue that a legal system with
direct authority over its subjects is not necessary for the existence of at
least some requirements of justice. Certain forms of global cooperation
are sufficient to generate some requirements of distributive justice even
if they are different from domestic basic structures in that they do not
involve political authority. One particular form of global cooperation
matches a main aspect of Freeman's characterisation of cooperative
schemes generating requirements of justice; there is a global property
system in at least some areas of international interaction, setting the
economic framework within which individuals and associations interact. Insofar as people cooperate in a global property system that sets
the economic framework for their actions, some requirements of justice
arguably apply among them. Recall the example of the global intellectual property rights regime in the pharmaceutical industry. I argued
that pharmaceutical research and development along the lines of the
TRIPs agreement represents a case of international rule-governed

cooperation. Participants follow and expect other participants to follow the rules of the property regime even assuming that there is no global political authority behind it. Furthermore, this cooperation significantly determines the economic framework for people worldwide and has pervasive effects on their life prospects. I concluded that this cooperation generates some requirements of distributive justice if not necessarily full-blown egalitarian requirements, such as Rawls's difference principle. These requirements can range from a greater inclusion of the global poor in decision-making mechanisms to showing greater concern for the interests of the worst off. In any case, the effect of the application of these requirements would be to reduce socio-economic inequalities.

Second, and more importantly, the objection fails even to show that Rawlsian principles of justice do not apply globally. There are globally valid egalitarian distributive requirements owing to the fact that global institutions with direct rule-making authority over individuals set the economic framework within which agents interact globally. Even though there is no unitary world state, there are arguably instances of global authority exercised by transnational institutions. Contrary to Freeman's claim, not all international institutions are fully voluntary agreements among sovereign governments that are entirely free to withdraw authority from these institutions at any time. In response to the political conception of justice, I have already discussed that Cohen and Sabel convincingly argue that non-compliance with, or exit from, institutions, such as the WTO and IMF, is prohibitively costly for member states. Furthermore, some global institutions have independent decision-making authority from member-state governments when they make, specify and apply rules. They exercise direct authority over individuals in member states because international rules are not necessarily mediated by member-state governments (Cohen and Sabel 2006). For this reason, international trade is not adequately characterised as a set of transactions governed by discrete agreements between sovereign governments; transnational institutions with global authority over individuals and associations set the economic framework within which these agents interact. In this respect, the global institutional system is much more akin to domestic basic structures than Freeman allows for. Global cooperation is relevantly similar to domestic. If so, arguably, there is a global basic structure that calls for the global application of Rawlsian principles of justice on the terms of the Rawlsian theory. The institutions of this basic structure have a profound effect on individual life prospects from the moment of birth for everyone subject to them; moreover, these institutions exercise political authority over individuals as they determine the economic and distributive framework within which they interact. Consequently, the global basic structure shaping the economic background against which transactions between agents take place must be structured in a fair way to allow for free interaction among parties and to preserve background justice.

I conclude that, from the assumption that egalitarian justice presupposes cooperation through political institutions, it does not follow that Rawlsian requirements of justice are limited to the domain of nation-states. It can be argued, however, that political institutions limit the scope of justice because of the role they play in its implementation. Political institutions can be necessary for justice, not only in the sense that justice presupposes existing institutions but also in the sense that political institutions are necessary for implementing the requirements of justice. It is thus the *feasibility* and not the *existence* of these institutions that matters for the existence of requirements of justice.[13] The scope of justice is limited to the range of persons whose cooperation could potentially be regulated by a common set of just political institutions. In this case, we can formulate the objection to the global extension of Rawlsian justice in the following way. Even though certain forms of global coordination and global authority profoundly affecting individual starting positions might currently exist, these are not sufficient for the application of any principle of justice with strong distributive implications, such as Rawls's two principles of justice. The political institutions of nation-states are necessary for the application of Rawlsian justice. Freeman argues that egalitarian justice is not feasible in the absence of a global state because, for principles of justice to be applicable, they must be authoritatively interpreted and enforced in the face of disagreement and opposition (Freeman 2006b: 253). One reason why this might be so is that politics is permanently characterised by pervasive disagreement. There is disagreement about what justice demands in terms of distribution because there is disagreement both about the appropriate principles of justice and about their correct interpretation. Political institutions are necessary to resolve disagreement, otherwise justice cannot be implemented because agents need assurance that other agents follow collectively just arrangements.[14] Nation-states are suited for this task because their governments claim the right authoritatively to settle debates about distributive justice, and to apply these decisions to their subjects. Using their monopoly of legitimate force, they will enforce laws even against those subjects who disagree with these. By contrast, no such centralised law-enforcement mechanism exists globally; thus, there is no political agent with authority to apply demanding principles of justice globally. Existing forms of global authority cannot provide assurance that global norms of egalitarian justice will be effectively enforced even against opposition by powerful governments. Short of global political institutions resembling those of nation-states, egalitarian justice cannot be implemented and thus the scope of Rawlsian justice is not global.

Charles Beitz argues that this objection is misconceived. He claims that showing that, at present, there are obstacles to implementing principles of Rawlsian justice is insufficient to prove that the principles do not apply globally. The present argument does not turn on whether or not a global basic structure capable of implementing Rawlsian principles of justice exists *now*. To show that Rawlsian principles of justice do not apply globally, it further needs to be proven that it is impossible to establish the required global institutions. If, however, the present obstacles to establishing the required global institutions are not fixed, cosmopolitan requirements of justice remain unaffected, and institutional design should take care of overcoming problems of implementation (Beitz 1999a: 156). Beitz also claims that there is no evidence that the lack of international political institutions amounts to an unalterable feature of the social world; hence, he concludes that the scope of justice is global (Beitz 1999a: 156–7). Even if at present there may not be political institutions at the international level that are capable of performing the same functions as domestic ones – most importantly, that of making and enforcing authoritative norms – such institutions can evolve in the future. Rawlsian principles of justice should be used to guide institutional reform at the global level to create just global institutions.

This argument is rather too quick, however. The claim about the feasibility of a just global basic structure needs to be justified. The lack of global political institutions can preclude the global application of Rawlsian principles of justice altogether if it is an unalterable fact of social life. To determine if principles of Rawlsian justice apply globally, we have to identify what features of political authority are necessary for their application, and we have to see if global political authority with the relevant features can be established. I will take up this task in Chapter 7. Nonetheless, Freeman's argument does not provide sufficient evidence to restrict the scope of Rawlsian justice to existing domestic political institutions.

5.3 COOPERATION AND THE STATE SYSTEM

I have evaluated three objections to globalising Rawlsian theory so far, which claimed that Rawlsian principles of justice do not apply globally because a global cooperation necessary for their application does not exist. Finally, let us consider the objection that the cooperation-based extension of Rawlsian theory to the global domain is too restrictive. Charles Beitz argues that, within a properly interpreted Rawlsian theory, global cooperation is not necessary for the existence of some global requirements of justice. Even in the absence of global cooperation there would be a case for global redistribution on the basis of the uneven distribution of natural resources among societies. He claims that parties in a global original position would adopt a resource redistribution principle for a scenario when all states are self-sufficient. This principle mandates the international redistribution of natural resources or the benefits deriving from their use (Beitz 1999a: 138). Beitz suggests that the argument for such a principle would be analogous to the informal argument Rawls gives for the two principles in *A Theory of Justice*, according to which the distribution of natural endowments is morally arbitrary, hence an unequal distribution of primary goods cannot be justified on the basis that they are deserved by the more talented. By analogy, Beitz argues that the global original position should reflect the view that some people's more advantageous location with respect to natural resources does not justify the exclusion of others from the benefits from these resources. These benefits must be fairly distributed globally even when there is no global economic cooperation.

Statists object to this suggestion in that it overlooks the fundamental role of social cooperation in giving rise to concerns of justice (Freeman 2006b). In the absence of a worldwide scheme of cooperation, there would simply be no occasion for a global original position that could yield principles for regulating the distribution of benefits from the use of natural resources among self-contained societies. The construct of the original position itself would not be valid for such a world. Rawls takes the scope of justice to be limited to those individuals who are fellow participants in a scheme of social cooperation. Because justice is a property of schemes of social cooperation, no requirements of distributive justice exist among persons not engaged in cooperation.

Cosmopolitans can give two different replies to this objection. The first type of answer remains within the Rawlsian framework. One can argue that, even though Beitz interprets cooperation in a more restricted sense, the state system itself represents a form of international cooperation sufficient to trigger Rawls's principles of justice, including the difference principle, for the global domain (Pogge 1989: 252). The system of territorial states with a property right or eminent domain over natural resources itself qualifies as a scheme of cooperation. In particular, states claim rights to exclude foreigners from access to resources within their territory, to control the use of non-private land and natural resources within their territory, and also to regulate the use of privately owned land and natural resources within their territory. Rights over resources crucially depend on social cooperation because they are defined by a set of rules that governs the utilisation of resources and determines the division of advantages and disadvantages among members of a society and non-members. Their effects on the individual life prospects of insiders and outsiders are profound and present from the start; thus, they stand in need of justification and are subject to assessment by the principles of justice. For instance, let us take the hypothetical case of coexisting self-sufficient societies sustaining themselves merely from the benefits of cooperation among their members, including the benefits from extracting the natural resources of their territory. According to the prevailing set of rules, all the benefits from natural resources go to the members of the society that extracted them, and outsiders receive nothing. There are, however, different available rules to govern internationally the ownership of, and control over, natural resources, including the distribution of benefits from the extraction of resources across societies. Which set of these rules is adopted makes a huge difference. The prevailing set of rules is not the only option and, in a Rawlsian framework, not even a privileged one serving as the natural baseline. From the fact that members of one society extract a certain quantity of natural resources, it does not follow that they are entitled to all the benefits from their use. Nor is it the case that societies automatically have a right to exclusive control over natural resources within their territory. There are alternative possible sets of rules that would regulate differently the division of advantages from the extraction of natural resources. For instance, a global resource tax could allocate a share of the benefits to those who are not members of the society that extracted them.[15] Any system of international rules governing the distribution of rights and duties with regard to the exploitation of natural resources, as well as the benefits and burdens from their use, represents a scheme of social cooperation. What rules govern the ownership of, and control over, natural resources should be decided by assessing alternatives in terms of the Rawlsian principles of justice, including the difference principle. Rather than triggering Beitz's resource-redistribution principle, international regimes governing the use of natural resources call for the application of Rawls's two principles of justice.

The second type of reply to the objection to natural-resource redistribution would concede that it is not demanded by Rawlsian theory because the state system itself does not amount to international cooperation in the sense required by the Rawlsian theory of justice. One could, however, argue directly for the conclusion that justice requires international redistribution on the basis of an equal claim held by every human being to a share of the Earth's resources. I shall consider this non-Rawlsian cosmopolitan argument in the following chapter.

5.4 SUMMARY AND CONCLUSION

This chapter presented an argument for the extension of the Rawlsian domestic theory of justice to the global domain. This cosmopolitan argument showed that there is a global basic structure relevantly similar to the domestic ones, and that the same reasons Rawls gives for the application of principles of justice within basic structures also hold for the global domain. Next, the chapter evaluated four objections to the global extension of the Rawlsian principles of justice that assume the validity of Rawlsian principles in the domestic case. The first three objections meant to show that there are relevant differences between the global domain and domestic societies which preclude the global application of Rawlsian principles of justice. These objections regarded the domestic and global domains:

1. different in degree, to the extent that the intensity of domestic cooperation is much greater than that of the global one;
2. different in kind because domestic societies amount to mutually beneficial cooperative schemes but global interaction does not;

3. different in kind because domestic cooperation is regulated by political institutions setting the economic framework within which agents interact.

Against these, I argued that:

1. there is global cooperation that takes place against the background of a global scheme of institutions and produces significant benefits and burdens, with unchosen and pervasive effects on the lives of most humans; thus, Rawlsian principles of justice should be applied to the global scheme of institutions so that the benefits and burdens of cooperation are fairly distributed;
2. the mutual-benefit criterion should not be used to determine the scope of justice because it would leave no room for evaluating unjust regimes, and, when it is used to select a distributive scheme from among the multiple available schemes to govern global cooperation, it favours Rawls's two principles of justice;
3. the scope of Rawlsian justice is not limited to nation-states even if it presupposes existing property regimes, and statists need to show that global political institutions necessary for the application of principles of justice cannot be established.

I argued that these objections do not warrant limiting the scope of Rawlsian principles of justice to domestic political institutions. The final objection argued that the cooperation-based extension of Rawlsian theory to the global domain is too restrictive, and that a resource redistribution principle applies in the absence of global cooperation. I replied that this conclusion does not follow on the terms of Rawlsian domestic theory, and that either Rawls's two principles of justice apply globally, because the territorial state system amounts to a scheme of cooperation in the relevant sense, or a non-Rawlsian argument is necessary to show that some requirements of distributive justice exist in the absence of cooperation. In what follows, I shall present a non-Rawlsian argument for global requirements of justice.

Notes

1 For a rich account of international interconnectedness, see Held and McGrew, 1999; Held and McGrew, 2000; Keohane, 2002.

2 For a seminal work on the subject see Keohane, 1984. See also Beitz, 1999, p. 148; Pogge 1989; Pogge 2002.
3 The argument was first elaborated by Charles Beitz, and the position was forcefully argued by Thomas Pogge (Beitz, 1999a; Pogge, 1989). The point was also made by Barry (1973) and Scanlon (1989). Beitz in a later article rejects the relevance of interconnectedness for the justification of demands of justice (Beitz, 1983, p. 595).
4 This point is argued in Risse, 2005b.
5 The example follows Beitz, 1999, p. 165.
6 For the pervasive effects of the global institutional scheme on individual lives see the rich account in Pogge, 2002.
7 The most elaborate argument to this effect is found in Pogge, 2002. See also O'Neill, 1974; Nagel, 1977.
8 For an argument to this effect see Risse, 2005a.
9 Another important condition Rawls includes in the definition is that the scheme must also be just.
10 For an argument to this effect see Moellendorf, 2002, pp. 72–4.
11 Various versions of the argument have been made by Miller, 2010, Samuel Freeman in Freeman, 2006a, and Freeman, 2006b, Thomas Nagel in Nagel, 2005, Michael Blake in Blake, 2001, and Debra Satz in Satz, 1999.
12 For the distinction between justice presupposing institutions and institutions being necessary for the implementation of justice see Abizadeh, 2007.
13 For the distinction between the two functions see Abizadeh, 2007.
14 For a more detailed argument see Chapter 7.
15 For such a proposal see Pogge, 1989; Pogge, 2002 pp. 196–215.

Chapter 6

NON-RELATIONAL COSMOPOLITAN THEORIES

In Chapter 5 we considered an argument for globalising Rawlsian justice. This cosmopolitan argument pointed out that the scope of justice is global because there is a global basic structure of economic institutions within which people interact throughout the world and which profoundly influences individual life prospects. Because this was a relational view that regarded existing cooperation within a basic structure as necessary for the existence of requirements of justice, the cosmopolitan conclusion depended on the factual assumption that the world as a whole is such a scheme of cooperation. The scope of requirements of justice was only contingently global because it depended on the existence of a global basic structure. In this chapter I shall look at some other, non-relational, reasons for holding that there are global requirements of justice.

We can describe non-relational views by contrasting them with relational theories. Relational conceptions of justice hold that individuals' standing in some specific practice-mediated relation – typically joint institutional membership – is a necessary condition for requirements of distributive justice to exist among them. To take two examples: political conceptions of justice regard joint subjection to the coercive institutions of a state as a necessary condition, whereas Rawlsians regard participation in consequential institutional schemes regulating social cooperation as necessary. Non-relational views, by contrast, do not regard institutions or other practice-mediated relations as necessary for the existence of requirements of justice. They claim that at least some demands of justice can emerge even in the absence of prior practice-mediated relations. Whether we have obligations of justice to others does not depend on whether we are fellow participants in an already existing common practice or subject to a common set of institutions.

To keep relational and non-relational views separate, it is important to emphasise that relational conceptions regard specific *prior practice-mediated* relations as necessary for grounding requirements of justice. Other kinds of relation, such as the relation of being in the position to assist someone in dire need, or the relation of being fellow humans, do not qualify as justice relation on the relational view. Thus, it is essential reference to prior practices that distinguishes relational from non-relational theories.

6.1 EQUAL RESPECT AND EQUAL TREATMENT

Like many ethical theories, non-relational cosmopolitanism is based on the view that all humans are of equal worth and their lives and well-being are equally important from the point of view of morality. It relies on a requirement of equal concern that we owe to all our fellow human beings by virtue of their status of being human. Cosmopolitans as well as many non-cosmopolitans share the moral outlook which holds that: only individual human beings have ultimate moral value; that all human beings have ultimate moral value; and that each human being has equal moral value.[1] This outlook rules out attaching ultimate moral value to other things, such as institutions, political communities, culture, relationships. It also forbids weighting the value of individuals differently in our moral thinking on the basis of features such as race, sex or ethnicity, as well as attaching no moral value at all to some human beings. Thus, it rules out racism as well as versions of nationalism that regard some groups of people as having no moral value or as having lesser value than others. This moral stance emphasises that persons deserve equal concern or respect regardless of differences between them. It does not necessarily favour non-relational theories over relational ones, however; we can accept its criteria and still hold that requirements of justice emerge only in certain practice-based relations. Thus, this outlook is compatible with a wide range of theories of justice, both cosmopolitan and statist. It is compatible, for example, with relational cosmopolitan theories that derive global requirements of justice from existing practice-mediated relations among all humans. It is also compatible with political conceptions of justice holding that requirements of justice apply only among a group of persons subject to common political authority. It can also accommodate some nationalist theories that allow us to give priority to our fellow nationals.

The requirement of equal concern, then, can be met by theories that require an equal treatment of all humans as well as by theories that do not.[2]

Non-relational cosmopolitan theories go beyond the requirement to accord equal respect to all humans, and hold that principles of justice require that all human beings be treated equally in some respect by individuals, groups or institutions.[3] Non-relational cosmopolitans regard the scope of justice as global because they think that our shared humanity is sufficient to give rise to the requirement of equal treatment. Our fellow humans are our equals; therefore, all humans – not only a subgroup of them – deserve equal treatment. Non-relational cosmopolitan theories of justice, however, are not necessarily egalitarian in distributive matters, in the sense of requiring the reduction of socio-economic inequalities. Besides egalitarian cosmopolitanism, various other non-relational cosmopolitan theories have been proposed, including utilitarian, libertarian, and sufficientarian cosmopolitanism. Each of these theories interprets differently the requirement of equal treatment. Utilitarians require treating everyone equally as a bearer of welfare and so an equal weighting of everyone's welfare in the utilitarian calculus, even though the actions or rules this requirement justifies do not assure equal outcomes in distribution, or even the reduction of socio-economic inequalities.[4] Libertarian cosmopolitans require treating everyone equally in the sense that our rights should be equally respected.[5] Sufficientarian cosmopolitans argue that everyone ought to have enough resources to satisfy their basic needs, or the resources one needs to become a fully functioning member of one's society, or the resources to fulfil our human capabilities.[6] Finally, there are those who advocate egalitarian requirements of global justice on non-relational grounds.[7] Non-relational egalitarians argue that equal respect requires that we treat all humans equally by limiting social and economic inequalities across the world. They regard our shared humanity as sufficient to justify certain egalitarian distributive requirements among all humans. Humans have competing claims over scarce natural and social goods which they need to fulfil their conceptions of the good. Egalitarian requirements of justice, limiting the range of permissible social inequalities, directly follow from the requirement to treat all humans equally. In what follows I shall evaluate three non-relational arguments for egalitarian requirements with a global scope.

6.2 GLOBAL CONTRACTUALISM

We saw earlier that Rawlsian cosmopolitans, such as Beitz and Pogge, justify the globalised application of Rawls's two principles of justice by employing the concept of a global original position. Fair principles of distributive justice are those that rational individuals would choose on the basis of their self-interest as a contractual agreement in an original position behind a veil of ignorance. Because the original position imagined by them includes representatives for everybody in the world, the contract which parties arrive at will determine requirements of distributive justice globally. The rationale Beitz and Pogge give for including representatives for every human being in this original position is that there is a global basic structure whose institutions regulate social and economic interaction among people worldwide, with profound effects on the life prospects of all. One might defend the idea of a global original position on different grounds, however, not relying on global interconnectedness via institutions as a necessary criterion for the existence of requirements of justice. A non-relational justification is offered by David A. J. Richards.[8] According to Richards, institutional interconnectedness is not a necessary condition for the global scope of justice; thus, it should not be used as a criterion for membership in a Rawlsian original position. It suffices for our inclusion in the original position that we are human beings. Following Rawls, Richards argues that there are two crucial characteristics of humans which make their interests the concern of justice: they have the capacity for an effective sense of justice; and also the capacity to form, revise, and pursue a conception of the good (Rawls 1999: 17; 442; Richards 1982; Beitz 1983: 595). These two powers of moral personality are possessed by all humans and this fundamental moral equality should be reflected by the principles of justice.[9]

   Why cannot institutional interconnectedness be a criterion for determining the scope of justice? The requirement to ignore our participation in institutional cooperation seems to follow naturally from Rawls's construction of the original position. Consider why Rawls thinks principles of justice should be derived behind a veil of ignorance which excludes information about parties' social background, their talents and skills, as well as their conception of the good life. The veil of ignorance is meant to exclude two sources of bias that can undermine the fairness of principles regulating social interaction. First, allowing the choice of principles to be guided by information about natural and social contingencies, such as talents, skills or social background, would permit factors that do not bear on people's possession of the two moral powers to influence improperly principles of justice. Personal features, such as one's sex, race, the social class of one's parents, and inborn natural endowments, should not play a role in justifying principles of justice because these principles ought to reflect the fundamental equality of humans. As Rawls formulates this point, these features are arbitrary from a moral point of view. Second, principles of justice should not be based on one's own particular idea of the good life because, if they were, we would choose principles of justice that allow us to exercise rights and freedoms important to us at the expense of rights and freedoms important to others. Rawls's two principles of justice are fair, then, because they reflect choices that do not systematically advantage one's own personal interests at the expense of other individuals who possess the same moral powers. Richards extends this reasoning to membership in institutional schemes. Participation in a scheme of cooperation should not determine what we owe to others as a matter of justice, so the argument goes, because it is just as arbitrary from a moral point of view as other personal characteristics that the veil of ignorance excludes, such as our intelligence, race or social background. Membership in institutional cooperation is a contingent matter that does not influence our possession of moral powers and that, for this reason, should not determine the choice of principles of justice. The original position reflects the fundamental equality of humans as moral persons. We are equals because we are all autonomous agents capable of thinking self-critically about our own lives as well as taking responsibility for them, and we are also capable of exercising our capacities that recognise the constraints of justice. So the only relevant criteria for including individuals in the original position where principles of justice are determined should be their possession of the essential powers of moral personality, that is, their capacity for an effective sense of justice and their capacity to form, revise, and pursue a conception of the good. Because all persons can be presumed to possess both powers of moral personality, whether or not they currently belong to a scheme of cooperation, all persons should be represented in the original position. The scope of justice is global, regardless of whether all humans participate in an institutionally regulated scheme of cooperation.

Furthermore, the requirements of justice endorsed by this argument are strongly cosmopolitan. Because parties' reasoning in the original position would be unchanged from the reasoning described in the cosmopolitan extension of Rawlsian justice, the principles chosen for the global domain would again be Rawls's two principles of justice. Parties in the global original position rationally choose principles on the basis of their self-interest behind a veil of ignorance. They do not know their socio-economic position and natural assets, nor do they have information about their membership in specific national political units, or whether the country in which they live is rich or poor. Under this radical uncertainty, parties would choose principles of justice that benefit the worst off because they would not be able to tell whether they will themselves end up in the worst-case scenario and they would want to maximise the prospects for this position. They would choose Rawls's two principles of justice, which secure an expansive set of rights and arrange material inequalities such that they benefit the poorest. Owing to the construction of the original position, the scope of the principles selected would be global. If we are barred from knowing which country we live in, we would accept principles of justice that allow only those socio-economic inequalities that benefit the globally worst off and that provide for fair equality of opportunity globally. The same egalitarian requirements of justice exist in the domestic and global domains.

This is a non-relational argument for global justice because it does not regard practice-mediated relations as necessary for the existence of requirements of distributive justice. It grounds requirements of distributive justice directly in the fundamental moral equality of persons. The features we possess which make our interests matter for justice are universal and do not depend on any contingent institutional relation with others. Thus, the revised global-original-position argument necessarily yields cosmopolitan principles of justice. Cosmopolitan requirements of justice will be as demanding as the requirements applying domestically.

6.3 EQUAL CLAIMS TO NATURAL RESOURCES

The second non-relational argument for global justice focuses on the distribution of natural resources. It holds that some requirements of justice exist outside practice-mediated relations because all humans have an equal claim to the Earth's natural resources. This equality of claims generates some requirements of justice with a global scope.

There are large inequalities in the global distribution of natural resources. Some countries, such as Saudi Arabia, are extremely rich in resources whereas others, such as Madagascar, are resource poor. Resource-rich countries derive large economic benefits from their natural resources. Economic inequalities resulting from differential access to natural resources must be justified. Some people's more advantageous location with respect to natural resources, however, does not in itself justify the exclusion of others from the benefits from these resources. As we saw in Chapter 5, for this reason Charles Beitz argued for a global resource redistribution principle. Beitz gives a Rawlsian argument for this principle, claiming that parties to a global original position would agree to it for a scenario when global cooperation is absent. There we also discussed the objection that a Rawlsian argument can never result in the acceptance of a resource redistribution principle either because the application of the original position would be invalid for a world without social cooperation or because parties would adopt Rawls's two principles of justice instead of the resource redistribution principle if we regard the territorial state system as a scheme of cooperation.

Cosmopolitans can give a different kind of argument for global redistribution on the basis of differential access to natural resources. The argument can be made that there are certain requirements of justice with a global scope that do not depend on the existence of global social cooperation. We can start out from the idea that no one has a better claim to the Earth's natural resources than anyone else, yet they are potentially valuable for everyone. Who will get the chance to make use of them, and how the benefits from their use should be distributed, should be justified. Because none of us has a better claim to natural resources than others, some cosmopolitans argue that all humans have an equal claim to them. The Earth belongs to all humans collectively, so our claims to resources should not depend on when and where we happened to be born. In some sense, our claims to natural resource are equal.[10]

We should clarify what it means to say that all humans have an equal claim to the Earth's resources, and what distributive requirements follow from this equality. The libertarian cosmopolitan Hillel Steiner argues that all of us have a right to an equal share of the monetary value of the Earth's natural resources and he thinks some fairly egalitarian international requirements of distributive justice are justified on this basis. Resource-rich countries should compensate resource-poor countries by contributing to a Global Fund which would administer the equal global per capita distribution of the value of natural resources. Further assuming that a substantial part of international economic inequalities results from unequal access to natural resources, Steiner argues that international requirements of distributive justice would significantly reduce global economic inequalities (Steiner 1994; Steiner 2005).

Steiner's argument for global distributive justice is based on libertarian ideas. For libertarians, justice requires respecting the rights of others, and nothing more. In particular, all of us have two basic rights others must respect: our rights of self-ownership over ourselves and our body; and our equal ownership rights over natural resources. All other moral rights we have can be derived from these two basic rights. According to libertarians a just social arrangement is one that ensures that these rights are respected and enforced. Redistributive transfers are required by distributive justice to redress the violations of ownership rights all humans have and to restore a just distribution. Steiner emphasises that violations of ownership rights in natural resources also generate some redistributive requirements of justice. We can acquire legitimate property rights over land and natural resources either by acquiring unowned land and resources or by the voluntary transfer of ownership title to us by the previous legitimate title holder. Both forms of acquisition must respect the rights of others, however. Most libertarians recognise moral limits on how one can appropriate land and resources, as they follow John Locke in holding that initial acquisitions of unowned resources must leave 'enough and as good' in common for others. Although this dictum can be interpreted as requiring that original appropriators leave for others enough and as good resources to appropriate, it is more plausible to require them to leave enough and as good resources for others to use. This requirement is satisfied by Steiner's position which holds that all humans have a right to an equal share of the monetary value of the aggregate of the world's natural resources. If someone appropriates unowned resources, one has a duty to transfer to others their share of the cash value of those resources as a condition of holding a legitimate title to them. Redistribution by monetary transfers then restores the justice of distributions in holdings.

Steiner's argument is cosmopolitan at its core because it allows for the existence of obligations of distributive justice to foreigners. After all, our violation of the property rights of others is not made less unjust by the fact that the victim is a foreigner. Everyone has the same rights regardless of where one lives, and state boundaries are irrelevant for our duties to redress rights violations. The purpose of international redistribution is to redress violations of individual property rights; thus it would be owed by persons to persons. Payments to and from the Global Fund, however, would be administered and enforced by states given the fact that the Earth's surface is divided up into territorial states claiming monopoly of force and exercising control over the natural resources within their territories. If they want to exercise their monopoly of force within their jurisdiction in a legitimate manner, states have a duty to enforce debt payments to the Global Fund by those residents who owe part of the cash value of their land and natural resource holdings to others. Furthermore, justice would require constant international transfers depending on the aggregate value of land in the world and its distribution across countries. Individual land-value entitlements depend on a number of factors, such as the global population size as well as on current technology, changing consumption patterns, depletions and discoveries of extractable resources.

Steiner's argument entails the strong cosmopolitan position that we have obligations of justice to foreigners and to our compatriots, and what we owe to the latter as a matter of justice is the same as what we owe to the former. Justice requires as much abroad as it does at home.[11] To what extent these obligations of justice would turn out to be egalitarian requirements is a matter of contention, however. Steiner thinks payments in and out of the Global Fund would be strongly redistributive because economic inequalities largely depend on unequal access to natural resources (Steiner 2005: 36). Assuming we include geographical location and climate among countries' resources, this claim would be in line with the findings of those social scientists who argue that the wealth or poverty of nations is primarily determined by their location and natural resources, including climate, soils, the availability of natural harbours and the prevalence of tropical diseases afflicting humans, other animals, and plants (Diamond 1999; Sachs 2001). If so, international requirements of justice would be fairly egalitarian because a large proportion of economic value would be redistributed across countries, leading to a substantial reduction of international socio-economic inequalities. Others argue, however, that natural resource endowments play no role in explaining inequalities across nations. What matters for prosperity are human factors, most importantly the quality of institutions, such as 'stable property rights, rule of law, bureaucratic capacity, appropriate regulatory structures to curtail at least the worst forms of fraud, anti-competitive behaviour, and graft, quality and independence of courts'.[12] If critics are right, global redistributive requirements, based on our collective ownership of the Earth's resources, would be minimal. Even though our obligations of distributive justice to foreigners are the same as our obligations of distributive justice to our compatriots, these are not substantial in either case. Neither international nor domestic requirements of justice would be very egalitarian.[13]

A further objection to Steiner's proposal is that our equal ownership of the Earth should not be interpreted as a right to an equal share of the value of the Earth's resources. Mathias Risse argues that our common ownership should rather be taken to mean that we all should have equal opportunity to satisfy our basic needs to the extent this depends on natural resources (Risse 2009: 288).[14] The reason why Risse thinks it is implausible that we should have a right to an equal share of the value of natural resources is that resources derive their value from human activities and social contexts in which different individuals participate to a different extent. For example, the market value of crude oil depends on the existence of markets and on factors influencing the demand for oil, such as the invention of internal combustion engine. The same quantity of raw materials can have vastly different values depending on these social factors. Furthermore, many resources require human labour to become available for production and exchange; they must be extracted, mined, processed, and so on. Their value depends largely on human labour. Risse concludes that our claims to a share of the value of resources are not equal then, because we are not symmetrically situated with respect to generating their value. Some of us are entitled to a larger share.

If Risse's argument appeals to the normative significance of desert individuals or societies acquire by contributing to the value of resources, it moves too swiftly, however. Granting that the value of natural resources depends on human factors and that our individual inputs are unequal, it does not follow that our entitlements to a share of the total value of resources must differ accordingly. An additional argument must be provided to show how individual value inputs relate to individual entitlements.

Our equal ownership of the Earth's resources can also be compatible with the moderate cosmopolitan position, according to which we have obligations of distributive justice both internationally and domestically, but domestic requirements of justice are more demanding. Instead of taking the libertarian position, which holds that obligations of justice are exhausted by respecting others' rights of self-ownership and equal ownership rights of natural resources, we might acknowledge that obligations of distributive justice arise on other grounds as well. For instance, cooperative schemes or political institutions might generate additional requirements of distributive justice beyond cosmopolitan requirements of justice deriving from our equal ownership of resources. International distributive requirements, entailed by our common ownership of natural resources, would then be a minimal baseline which could be exceeded by more egalitarian domestic obligations.

Nonetheless, even if they do not determine the content of justice by permitting deviations from equality on the basis of desert or by generating egalitarian distributive requirements which supplement less demanding distributive obligations humans owe one another as co-owners of natural resources, institutions can determine the content of justice by specifying the meaning of distributive equality. Consider the following two ways our common ownership of the Earth's resources can require political and economic institutions.

First, discussion of humans' common ownership may be meaningless if ownership rights are entirely conventional and require an elaborate set of political and economic institutions for their existence. There are then no natural – that is, pre-institutional – ownership rights, and ownership is defined within political systems. In the absence of political and economic institutions, no obligations of distributive justice could be based on our ownership of the world and of ourselves.

Second, even if it makes sense to talk about ownership in abstraction from existing institutions, we may not know what it means to have an *equal* ownership of the Earth's resources without institutions. The monetary value of resources may not be determined in this case. For instance, markets can be necessary to specify the value of land and natural resources because these goods can be used for multiple purposes and individuals' preferences over them vary. If so, institutions define what a just distribution is. In Chapter 7, I shall argue in more detail that institutions partially constitute the content of justice by determining fair distributive shares as well as requirements of justice for individuals.

To conclude, if the Earth's resources belong to humankind in common, our common ownership of the Earth's resources gives rise to some requirements of justice with a global scope. How much these requirements demand of us depends on a number of factors, such as how our common ownership of the Earth should be interpreted and whether inequalities in natural resource endowments have a causal role to play in generating socio-economic inequalities. Depending on these, the requirements may be moderate, with limited international distributive obligations, or egalitarian, with substantial reduction in socio-economic inequalities.

6.4 LUCK EGALITARIAN COSMOPOLITANISM

Luck egalitarians argue that institutional relational facts, such as one's citizenship or country of residence, should play no role in justifying socio-economic inequalities. They hold that it is unfair for one person to be worse off than another through no fault of his/her own. Distributive differences among individuals should reflect only the choices of individuals themselves and should not reflect their unchosen social circumstances or natural endowments. Thus, the task of distributive justice is to correct for disadvantages that individuals have due to factors beyond their control. Cosmopolitan requirements of justice can be derived from luck egalitarianism. Because one's citizenship or country of residence is not determined by one's own choice, it is unfair for someone to be worse off than another person because of these contingencies. Distributive justice requires correcting for international inequalities.

As we saw in Chapter 4, luck egalitarianism is a prominent version of contemporary egalitarianism. Is it a plausible position, though? To see this, we need to go back to what many consider the starting point of this theory. Luck egalitarianism was inspired by John Rawls's theory even though Rawls rejects luck egalitarianism, or what he calls 'the principle of redress', as a theory of justice (Rawls 1999a: 86–7). What luck egalitarians emphasise in Rawlsian theory is the intuitive case Rawls makes in defence of his principles of justice. Rawls motivates his argument for his second principle by pointing out that inequalities in people's life prospects are often caused by factors that cannot play a normative role in justifying principles of justice, such as sex, race, the social class of their parents, and their inborn natural endowments. As Rawls formulates it, these sources of inequality are morally arbitrary

(Rawls 1999a: Chapter II). Because they are so arbitrary, the distribution of resources should not be allowed 'to be improperly influenced' by them (Rawls 1999a: 63). Luck egalitarians interpret Rawls's reference to moral arbitrariness as suggesting that egalitarian justice properly interpreted is based on a requirement to equalise those interpersonal inequalities that cannot be traced back to voluntary individual choices, and only inequalities resulting from voluntary individual choices are justified (Arneson 1989; Dworkin 2000; Cohen 1989).[15] The underlying idea is that there is a morally significant difference between inequalities resulting from people's choices and inequalities that are non-voluntary. For instance, Ronald Dworkin, one of the earliest proponents of luck egalitarianism, argues for a theory of egalitarian justice that prescribes a distribution of resources that is endowment insensitive and ambition sensitive: a theory that makes people's holdings depend on their choices but not on their natural endowments or other unchosen circumstances (Dworkin 2000: 89). Luck egalitarians view inequalities which are beyond our control as not merely unfortunate but unfair. A natural and social lottery assigns to us starting positions at our birth determining our life chances, and we end up winners or losers in this lottery through no fault of our own. These inequalities are often glaring and, if we focus on their causes, we are drawn towards the intuition that they are unjust. For example, many of us consider differences in the colour of one's skin, one's religion, gender, and ethnicity, or mere physical distance as features that we must ignore if we are to pay equal respect to others. Luck egalitarians believe that distributive justice demands the equal treatment of the interests of everybody, in the sense that we should not let these differences influence socio-economic inequalities.

This intuition draws support from the important place modern societies attribute to equality of opportunity in regulating competition for jobs and offices. Social and economic life is full of competitions where we compete for valuable prizes, such as jobs, political positions and other social goods. The idea of equal opportunity is meant to ensure that the terms of competition are fair and that winners and losers have been treated equally. Historically, calls for equality of opportunity initially demanded the elimination of legal and quasi-legal barriers to various socially desirable goods, such as jobs, offices, access to political participation and public goods and services. The idea was that contestants should be judged on the basis of their skills and talents and not on the basis of irrelevant traits such as class background, religion, race, ethnicity, gender and sexual orientation. This idea provided the foundation for anti-discrimination legislation in the United States and in other countries. Later, however, the requirement of equal opportunity extended to other social and educational measures counteracting the effects of past injustices such as racism, gender bias, and class privilege. These measures together ensure that equality of opportunity prevents some morally arbitrary contingencies, such as class or race, from determining individual life chances. Luck egalitarians, however, claim these measures do not go far enough; they permit the distribution of natural traits, such as talents and skills, including intelligence, determination and diligence, to determine distributive inequalities. Those with few marketable talents and skills end up on the losing side. Luck egalitarians regard these features as morally arbitrary to the same extent, and argue that justice requires the elimination of distributive inequalities resulting from these factors as well. The extent to which we possess certain talents and skills is typically not the result of our own choices. Just as social contingencies, such as birth into a family and its social position, can be regarded as the outcome of a social lottery, luck egalitarians regard natural contingencies as the outcome of a natural lottery which are just as arbitrary from a moral point of view. Justice requires redressing both social and natural contingencies because none of these reflects our individual choices. Luck egalitarianism, then, goes beyond Rawls's principles of justice. Rawls's principles require equal opportunity for persons with different social backgrounds but they still permit inequalities on the basis of natural traits, provided that these inequalities benefit the worst off. Luck egalitarians demand the complete elimination of these inequalities.

It seems natural to extend luck egalitarianism to the global domain. Nationality seems to belong to the same family as the characteristics listed above. Surely, it seems no less arbitrary to have significantly lower life prospects just because one is born into a poor rather than a rich country than it is arbitrary to have poorer life prospects than others in the same country because of the wealth of one's parents. Neither of these inequalities is a matter of individual choice. If unchosen causes of inequality are objectionable domestically, they seem just as objectionable internationally (Moellendorf 2002; Caney 2005). The place where one is born is perhaps the most important factor determining what prospects we face at birth for our entire life. As we saw in the

Introduction, there are enormous economic inequalities between affluent and poor regions in the world. The poorest half of the world's population consumes only a tiny fraction of that which the richest 15 per cent does.[16] Economic inequalities are coupled with huge inequalities in the life prospects of individuals. Average life expectancy in Africa is around twenty-five years shorter than in the Americas or Europe and, in the poorest countries, it barely reaches half of the life expectancy in some of the richest ones.[17] The most striking differences concern the prospects faced by children under the age of five in the poorest and the wealthiest countries. If born in one of the least developed countries, one has a significantly greater probability of dying before reaching the age of five than someone born in one of the high-income countries.[18] For example, a child born in Mali has a sixty times higher chance of dying before the age of five than a child born in Norway (World Bank 2011). International inequalities in life prospects can be explained to a large extent by unequal access to food and basic health care. In poor countries, we can often find rates of under-five malnutrition of 30 to 40 per cent. As an FAO (Food and Agriculture Organization of the United Nations) report puts it, 'two out of five children in the developing world are stunted, one in three is underweight and one in ten is wasted' (FAO 1999: 11, quoted in Pogge 2002: 97), while children in developed countries do not have to face such grim prospects for their lives. Most people would consider similar inequalities unjust if they arose between citizens of the same country. Furthermore, international inequalities cannot be attributed to individual choices that could make the poor responsible for their plight. The only difference that could explain the different prospects of two children – one born in Mali, the other in Norway – seems to be the personal luck of having been born in one of these countries, rather than in the other. These are vast inequalities in individual life prospects for which these individuals themselves are not responsible. Luck egalitarians regard them as not merely unfortunate but unjust because they are generated to a large extent by factors that are beyond individual control, and which thus violate the requirement of equal treatment. Cosmopolitan luck egalitarians thus argue that global distributive differences should not reflect these unchosen features; distributive justice should eliminate inequalities resulting from them.

Because luck egalitarianism is a non-relational theory, abstracting from all institutional or cultural ties that might hold among people, national borders seem to be irrelevant for our obligations of justice. If nationality is just as arbitrary from a moral point of view as the colour of our hair, our sex, or the social class of our parents, it should play no role in determining what we owe each other as a matter of distributive justice. Not only do luck egalitarian requirements of justice have a global scope, our obligations of justice towards our compatriots are the same as our obligations of justice towards foreigners. These requirements could turn out to be very demanding given the fact that socio-economic inequalities are influenced to a large extent by factors for which individuals are not responsible. First, they would require redistribution on the basis of differential access to external goods such as natural resources. Furthermore, redistribution would be due on the basis of economic inequalities resulting from an unequal access to cultural goods, such as technology, language, art, education, and so on, which are also beyond individual control. Finally, radical redistributive implications can potentially follow from our differential endowment with natural assets, such as genetic material, that are unchosen and have a substantial role in determining our lifetime distributive shares.

We may have several reasons to resist the cosmopolitan egalitarian distributive requirements that luck egalitarians defend. Some of these criticisms are not specific to cosmopolitan versions of luck egalitarianism. The luck egalitarian ideal has been heavily criticised in the domestic case both by critics of egalitarianism and by egalitarians. First of all, egalitarianism has traditionally been subject to widespread external criticism by non-egalitarians.[19] Critics have argued, for instance, that the pursuit of equality is futile because there is an endless variety among individuals as a result of which no two individuals are really equal; the diversity of individual talents, ambitions, social identities, and circumstances ensures that any attempt to achieve equality in some dimension will inevitably generate inequality in others (Hayek 1960: 87). Others object to the pursuit of equality on the ground that it is wasteful because egalitarianism would require throwing away external goods that cannot be evenly divided rather than letting some people have more than others.[20] Even worse, it may require levelling down people's talents and abilities when they cannot be lifted to the same level (Nozick 1974: 229). More recently, debates internal to egalitarianism have become prominent; some egalitarians have claimed that luck egalitarianism is an indefensible version of egalitarianism.[21] These critics argue that applying the choice–luck distinction to issues of distributive justice is both philosophically implausible and morally unappealing. First, it might be impossible to disentangle those factors influencing our distributive shares that are the result of our voluntary choices from those that are not. Choices we consider voluntary are often influenced by our unchosen features, such as genetic make-up or social environment (Scheffler 2003b). Second, to many, it seems morally unpalatable that luck egalitarians would fully compensate us for disadvantages resulting from unchosen factors but would deny assistance to those disadvantaged through their own voluntary choices. Critics argue that luck egalitarianism would require abandoning suffering or dying patients whose misfortune is the result of their own imprudent or risky choices (Anderson 1999). I will set aside these general criticisms of luck egalitarianism and focus instead on criticisms of its cosmopolitan version. Assuming luck egalitarianism is a plausible position for domestic justice, are there any reasons against adopting egalitarian requirements for the global domain on luck egalitarian grounds?

According to one strand of criticism, nationality is not morally arbitrary in the same sense as one's sex, skin colour or the class of one's parents are. There is a morally relevant difference between nationality and these features. I will consider two reasons why this might be so. First, granting that morally arbitrary inequalities should not be reflected in distributive arrangements, one can argue that cosmopolitan luck egalitarians misdescribe what moral arbitrariness means. If we think of nationality as a set of relationships in which we stand with others, rather than merely as one of our individual features we are not responsible for, it may seem less arbitrary than cosmopolitan luck egalitarians claim. Standing in certain kinds of relationship with others can be morally relevant, that is, not arbitrary, and it can give rise to special distributive requirements to people with whom we are fellow participants. This point can be spelled out as follows. There are two different senses of moral arbitrariness which luck egalitarians conflate. In one sense, we can regard those, and only those, individual features as morally arbitrary for which the person in question is not responsible. Nationality would be arbitrary in this sense, because we are typically born into a nation without being given the opportunity to have a choice about membership and about the advantages and disadvantages that come with it. In a different sense, however, moral arbitrariness means simply the normative conclusion that certain properties of persons should not be allowed to influence the way they are treated. Luck egalitarians identify the two meanings without justification; they assume the truth of a further premise that features of persons for which they are not themselves responsible should not make a difference to how they are treated.[22] This premise, however, is not obviously true. As relational conceptions of justice emphasise, there might be various kinds of unchosen relationship in which we stand with others that can make a difference to what we owe them. Political conceptions of justice hold that being fellow citizens, subject to the same set of coercive political institutions, is a normatively relevant relation, making a significant difference to our requirements of justice. For Rawlsians, it is our mutual interaction with others through cooperative institutions, or our causal interconnectedness, that makes a difference to our distributive obligations. Whatever the merits of these conceptions, they show that there are arguments for the claim that special relationships generate special obligations. Luck egalitarians cannot simply assume the opposite – so the objection goes – they must provide an argument for it (Daniels 2008: 339). Note, however, that this is not an objection to the cosmopolitan version of luck egalitarianism but to luck egalitarianism as such. It argues that luck egalitarianism is wrong to identify morally arbitrary considerations with features for which individuals are not responsible. If, however, all unchosen features are morally arbitrary and nationality is indeed an unchosen feature, it follows that nationality is a morally arbitrary fact that should not be reflected in international socio-economic inequalities.

There is a second reason why nationality might not be morally arbitrary, that is, why it may be relevant for determining distributive obligations. Even if luck egalitarians are right to claim that unchosen features of a person should not influence his/her distributive shares, international distributive inequalities may not be unchosen. Recall that luck egalitarians hold that individuals should be held responsible for their circumstances if these result from their voluntary choices, however imprudent or unwise they may have been. Smith is not required to compensate Jones for his relative disadvantage if Jones is worse off than Smith because he has chosen surfing over working hard. If persons can be held responsible for how they fare relative to people in other countries, international distributive inequalities are arguably not unjust insofar as they are not based on morally arbitrary features. Whether or not this is so depends on how much our countries' economic standing is the result of our own individual choices. As we saw in Chapter 4, Rawls and others regard members of nations responsible for their nations' wealth or poverty because they think our choices determine the economic and social policies of our nations. We can be regarded as responsible for our nations' social and economic policies if we have voted for them. Even when we did not, we may be regarded as responsible for them if we have a genuine choice to emigrate. If these policies were within our control and as a result of them we end up worse off than people in other countries, we have no claims of justice against these people to eliminate distributive inequalities between us and them. Nationality can be morally relevant in the sense that it circumscribes a group of people that can be held responsible for the relative economic standing of their country. In response to this point, I argued that the conditions necessary for holding citizens responsible for their countries' economic standing do not usually hold. Global poverty is caused to a substantial extent by external factors rather than by domestic causes within developing countries. Furthermore, members of political communities cannot be treated as agents responsible for their governments' policies and liable for their results in the case of non-democratic societies, dissident minorities and future generations. To the extent that we cannot be held responsible for our countries' relative economic standing, cosmopolitan luck egalitarianism would justify substantial global redistribution in the face of current global inequalities.

It is time to sum up the objections to cosmopolitan luck egalitarianism we have discussed. The two objections I discussed targeted the cosmopolitan claim that nationality is a morally arbitrary fact which cannot give rise to differential distributive requirements. Nationality may not be morally arbitrary either because not all unchosen factors are morally irrelevant or because, even if they are, the choices made by fellow nationals might make them responsible for their country's wealth or poverty. In response to the first point, I noted that the objection is not specific to the cosmopolitan version of luck egalitarianism but is an objection to luck egalitarianism as such. In response to the second point, I have argued that, if we grant to luck egalitarians that all unchosen features are morally arbitrary and thus should not influence distributive outcomes, nationality does not make a difference to what we owe to others abroad because most of us cannot be held responsible for how our own country fares relative to others.

6.5 SUMMARY AND CONCLUSION

I have evaluated three non-relational arguments for the claim that the scope of distributive justice is global. These arguments were non-relational because they do not regard prior practice-mediated relations as necessary for the existence of requirements of justice. They regard our common humanity as sufficient to generate global distributive requirements. Contrary to how Rawls and Rawlsians see it, the scope of justice is not limited to fellow members in institutional schemes. All three arguments concluded that global requirements of justice are the same as domestic ones. The extent of global redistribution they sanction varies, however. Global contractualism can justify Rawls's two principles of justice for the global domain and thus it is likely to generate substantial global redistributive obligations. The libertarian interpretation of our common ownership of the Earth gives rise to the same redistributive requirements globally and domestically but whether or not these are going to be egalitarian depends on how to interpret the statement that we own the Earth's resources in common and on the degree natural-resource endowments contribute to socio-economic inequalities. Finally, global luck egalitarianism justifies the requirement to equalise unchosen inequalities both domestically and globally but the extent of global – and domestic – redistribution will depend on the extent to which we are responsible for our economic circumstances.

Notes

1   One can regard these characteristics as necessary elements of the cosmopolitan outlook, as Pogge (2002, p. 169), Barry (1999, pp. 35–6), and others do. As I argue below, however, these characteristics are compatible with theories that are not cosmopolitan about distributive justice.

2   To avoid misunderstandings, I need to emphasise the distinction between the claim that individuals are of *equal moral value* or *concern* and the requirement of *equal treatment*. Relational views are distinguished by conditioning the latter requirement, that of equal treatment, on specific relations among individuals. They need not so condition, however, attributing equal moral value or concern to all humans.

3   This formulation deliberately leaves open the question of whether principles of justice apply to individual conduct, group decisions, or the design of institutions. That is, it is compatible with competing positions about the *site* of distributive justice.

4 Utilitarian cosmopolitans include Peter Singer and Peter Unger. See Singer, 1972; Unger, 1996.

5 A version of libertarian cosmopolitanism was proposed by Hillel Steiner. See Steiner, 1994.

6 See the works of Elizabeth Anderson, Martha Nussbaum, and Amartya Sen for the sufficientarian view (Anderson, 1999; Nussbaum, 2000; Sen, 1992).

7 Non-relational egalitarian cosmopolitanism is represented by David Richards, Allen Buchanan, Onora O'Neill, Simon Caney, among others. See Richards, 1982; Buchanan, 2003; O'Neill, 2000; Caney, 2005.

8 The argument was also endorsed by Charles Beitz in an article published subsequent to the publication of *Political Theory and International Relations* (Richards, 1982; Beitz, 1983).

9 More precisely, the two moral powers are possessed by almost all humans. Rawls allows for some marginal individual cases when individuals lack these capacities (Rawls, 1999a, p. 443).

10 This cosmopolitan stance goes back at least to Hugo Grotius's *Three Books on the Law of War and Peace* (published in 1625) (Grotius, 2005). It was also famously endorsed by Immanuel Kant who says in *Perpetual Peace* that humans own the Earth in common (Kant, 1992, p. 106).

11 On this view, we may have other, e.g. patriotic or familial, moral obligations that do not have global scope. These are not requirements of justice, however, as they do not correspond to any correlative right (Steiner, 1994, p. 262).

12 Risse (2005c, p. 355) refers to numerous sources in the literature.

13 In the latter case, Steiner's theory would imply that some very poor countries that are rich in natural resources would have to compensate some very rich but otherwise resource-poor countries. Many might find this conclusion unappealing. No such counter-intuitive redistributive requirements would obtain, however, if the key determinant of a country's relative economic standing is access to natural resources.

14 Risse argues that no international redistributive obligations follow from this requirement because it is not the case that cross-country economic inequalities are determined by countries' relative natural resource endowments. He believes that international inequalities are determined by the quality of institutions (Risse, 2005a, 2005b, 2005c).

15 There is some textual support for luck egalitarianism in Rawls's work. For example, in the 1971 edition of *A Theory of Justice*, Rawls claims that his conception of justice 'nullifies the accidents of natural endowment and the contingencies of social circumstance as counters in [a] quest for political and economic advantage' (Rawls, 1971, p. 15). As we shall see, luck egalitarianism is heavily contested even by some egalitarians. It has been

challenged in, for example, Anderson, 1999; Scheffler, 2003b; Daniels, 2003.

16 Recall that 44 per cent of the world's population – those living below the $2 a day international poverty line – consume only 1.3 per cent of the global product, whereas the high-income countries, with 15 per cent of the global population, consume about 81 per cent of it (World Bank, 2003, p. 235).

17 Forty *v.* eighty+ years (Daniels, 2008, p. 325).

18 The ratio is more than 25 to 1 (UNICEF, 2006).

19 See, for instance, Hayek, 1960; Nozick, 1974; Raz, 1986.

20 See the 'levelling down objection' of Joseph Raz in Raz, 1986, p. 227.

21 The term 'luck egalitarianism' itself was coined by Elizabeth Anderson who provided a powerful critique of the theory in Anderson, 1999. Similar critiques have been made by, among others, Samuel Scheffler in Scheffler, 2003b and Jonathan Wolff in Wolff, 1998.

22 For a clear description of the two senses of moral arbitrariness, and the need to keep them separate, see Miller, 2005.

Chapter 7

INSTITUTIONS AND THE APPLICATION OF PRINCIPLES OF JUSTICE

I started the book by asking a number of questions about global justice. Do we have a duty of justice to contribute to eradicating global poverty and to reducing inequalities? If so, can we apply globally the principles of justice we accept for the domestic domain? One may think that these questions can be answered automatically by taking a stance on the debate between cosmopolitans and statists. I argue in this chapter that answers in this controversy do not automatically settle questions of justice about global distributive issues even when there is agreement about the principles of justice. Even if we start out with a cosmopolitan conception of justice, there are reasons why its distributive principles might not be applicable to certain global distributive questions, if we suppose that their application requires that they should be capable of evaluating distributions and guiding individual action and institutional design. In the course of the argument, I explore the role of economic and political institutions in determining the content of principles of justice, and the way this constrains the applicability of principles of justice.[1] This chapter is structured as follows. First, I outline a version of the cosmopolitan position which is based on a non-relational view of justice. I then show that it does not follow from the non-relational view that principles of distributive justice can be applied to adjudicate distributive questions globally. I argue that, in the absence of political and economic institutions, under certain conditions, principles of justice are not determinate enough to define fair individual distributive shares, and even if they could do so, they are not determinate enough to guide individual conduct with regard to justice. Therefore, I argue that existing institutions may delimit the scope of application of principles of justice. They do not represent the outer bounds of justice, however, because the global institutional set-up can be reformed so as to become more sensitive to the demands of global justice. The chapter's argument illuminates one sense in which the institutions and policies Rawls covers by the term basic structure are special.[2]

7.1 RELATIONAL AND NON-RELATIONAL THEORIES OF JUSTICE

In the previous chapters I evaluated various statist and cosmopolitan positions on global justice. Cosmopolitans and statists disagree about the scope of justice, that is, about the range of persons who owe one another responsibilities of distributive justice. Cosmopolitans hold that the scope of distributive justice is global. Statists, by contrast, argue that the scope of distributive justice is limited to citizens of the same state. I approached these theories by looking at the role they accord to political and economic institutions in grounding justice, and I analysed their implications for the scope of justice. In particular, I have distinguished relational and non-relational conceptions of justice. Relational conceptions of justice hold that individuals' standing in a specific practice-mediated relation is a necessary condition for requirements of distributive justice to exist among them. These relations are typically taken to correspond to institutions and policies that regulate social and economic inequalities, most importantly 'the political constitution and principal economic and social arrangements' covering domains such as legal rules of property and the organisation of the economy.[3] These institutions have been regarded as necessary for the existence of justice relation under three descriptions: as having a profound and pervasive effect on the lives of their subjects; as employing coercive force against their subjects; or as authoritatively governing cooperative schemes among their participants.[4] As I have referred to it, relational theories regard these relations as playing a *foundational* role in grounding requirements of justice.

Non-relational views deny this. They claim that at least some demands of justice can emerge even in the absence of practice-mediated relations. Political or economic institutions do not ground all requirements of justice.

The disagreement between relational and non-relational conceptions of justice can motivate different views about the scope of justice. If we subscribe to the relational view, the scope of justice will be contingent on the kinds of relation we stand in with others. Absent the requisite relation at the global level and there will be no global requirements of justice. If, however, we hold a non-relational view of justice, then we have a strong case for the global scope of justice. Non-relational theories are cosmopolitan.[5] They allow for demands of justice to exist even in the absence of practice-mediated relationships. At first glance, this seems to imply that principles of justice contained by non-relational conceptions should automatically be applicable to adjudicating globally arising distributive issues and that non-relational theories are committed to a requirement of global redistribution on the basis of justice.[6]

This chapter concerns the inference drawn from non-relational theory to the global applicability of the principles of justice. I will show that it does not follow from the non-relational view, or indeed from any other cosmopolitan egalitarian position, that principles of distributive justice can be applied with a global scope to all arising distributive issues. Institutions can affect the scope of application of principles of justice even when they do not give rise to them.

7.2 THE APPLICATION OF PRINCIPLES OF JUSTICE

For the sake of argument, suppose we hold a non-relational egalitarian view of distributive justice. To keep the argument applicable to a fairly broad range of egalitarian theories, let us suppose we accept a principle of justice that prescribes that resources must be distributed in a way that limits the range of socio-economic inequalities among individuals.[7] Does it follow from the non-relational outlook that this principle can be applied to adjudicate distributive questions globally?

We should clarify what it means to say that principles of distributive justice have a global application. It seems plausible to hold as a necessary condition for principles of justice to be applicable at a certain time that they should be capable of assessing states of affairs, guiding and evaluating individual action and/or institutional design with regard to a just distribution at that time.[8] In other words, to be applicable, principles of justice must enable judgements about the justice or injustice of distributions, actions or institutions. Thus, they can have global application only if they can do so with regard to a globally just distribution for the agents and institutions concerned. If we understand the application of principles in this sense, non-relational cosmopolitan theories prescribing a global egalitarian distribution do not imply that egalitarian distributive principles can be applied to all globally arising distributive issues. It does not follow from them, for example, that we individually should redistribute our surplus resources to those who are worse off.

To see why, let us distinguish between three different functions that institutions can play in a theory of justice. They can be regarded as having a role in grounding requirements of justice; in implementing the pre-institutional content of distributive principles; and in constitutively determining the content of principles. The first function is emphasised by relational theories which attribute a foundational role to institutions. The standard view of institutions focuses on the second function. I shall defend the third one. We shall shortly see that institutions partly constitute the content of principles of justice. These principles do not define a fair distribution or a set of requirements for individuals antecedently to, and independently from, the rules making up the institution. Because these principles do not yield a sufficiently determinate standard for assessing distributions and for guiding and evaluating actions and institutional design, they may not be applied to adjudicate distributive matters outside existing institutions.

7.3 INSTITUTIONS AS EFFECTIVE INSTRUMENTS TO ACHIEVE JUSTICE

Before I defend in detail the constitutive view of institutions, let me briefly outline what I take to be the standard view. This view regards institutions as merely the most effective instruments to carry out justice-based requirements, defined independently from the rules of existing institutions. They are instrumental in overcoming the short-comings of moral agents in performing their duties. This view would have the following justification.

Suppose the content of principles of justice can be fully determined in abstraction from the rules of actual institutions. Individuals are to contribute to a fair distribution of resources by reducing socio-economic inequalities where fair shares can be fully specified without reference to institutional rules. In complex societies, however, it would be very difficult for an individual, left to his/her own devices, to know exactly how to act in order contribute his/her fair share. To know what to do, we have to have access to all sorts of relevant information, such as that about the current distribution and the expected effects of all possible courses of action available to us, possibly leading into the indefinite future. Because of insuperable informational and cognitive limitations, individual actions aiming at justice could approximate it only imperfectly. Justice can be promoted more effectively by creating and maintaining just institutions, that is, systems of rules following which is more likely to result in a just distribution than could independent individual actions. For instance, a social division of labour, involving experts with special skills or knowledge, and the assignment of special rights and responsibilities, might make attempts to pursue justice more effective.

A version of this argument can be constructed following Rawls's remarks about the function of the basic structure. Rawls argues that, because of the impact individual actions have on the lives of a large number of individuals through a long-term horizon, individuals cannot realistically be required to foresee all the ramifications of their actions, and so they cannot be charged with the performance of principles of distributive justice (Rawls 1993a: 266–9).[9] The institutions of the basic structure can make the necessary adjustments to maintain background justice which individuals cannot. For this reason, he argues, the proper site of distributive justice is the basic structure of society in the sense that primary principles of justice apply to the authoritative institutions of the basic structure only; they do not apply, however, to individual actions or even to institutions taken individually. This epistemological case is certainly one reason why institutions are important for distributive justice. I explain below, however, that the institutions of the basic structure are special for justice in a further sense. They would be required even if individuals were blessed with perfect foresight and spotless cognitive capacities. There are two general reasons for this. One is rooted in the indeterminacy of fair distributive shares; the other is due to the strategic character of human interaction. Under any plausible egalitarian conception, fundamental principles of justice underdetermine both what fair individual shares are and what individuals ought to do with regard to justice.

In what follows, I shall present an alternative conception of institutions in which they are not merely seen as instruments of the performance of justice-based requirements individuals have, defined independently from, and prior to, the rules of institutions. The institutions of the basic structure are central for distributive justice by performing two further functions: first, economic markets and political institutions are necessary for defining a just distribution; second, political institutions are also necessary for determining the content of requirements of justice by regulating strategic interaction between individuals, thus determining the underdetermined content of requirements. I shall now look at economic markets and political institutions in turn.

7.4 MARKET INSTITUTIONS IN RESOURCE EGALITARIANISM

One reason why institutions may be indispensable for the applicability of principles of justice to actual distributive issues is that markets may be essential for determining the value of resources to be distributed in accordance with principles of justice, and thus for defining fair distributive shares. This is the case, for instance, in those theories of distributive justice that rely on market mechanisms in determining the value of resources which are to be allocated.

Ronald Dworkin argues that egalitarian justice requires the equal distribution of resources. Consequently, in Dworkin's theory, the content of requirements of justice is partially defined by markets that enable transactions between individuals. To be able to arrive at a just distribution of resources – equality of resources, as Dworkin terms his conception – we need the operation of markets to determine the value of resource bundles belonging to individuals. In the absence of markets, there is simply no way to tell what an individual's fair share of resources is. Consider the following reason. Resources, which distributive justice is in the business of distributing, are very heterogeneous, and individuals assign differing values to them. To overcome the problem of determining an interpersonally comparable value to these resources, Dworkin proposes a thought experiment, in which people, using a token currency distributed equally at the outset, participate in a series of auctions until everybody has such holdings that nobody envies anybody else's bundle of goods. At this point, we can say that everyone has an equal share of resources, Dworkin argues (Dworkin 2000: 71–2). For this reason, in devising redistributive institutions, governments should aim to mimic fair and efficient market mechanisms that define fair distributive shares. Market institutions are seen here not only as effective instruments in securing a just outcome that can be defined independently from them. They define what a just distribution is.

Even though Dworkin presents the series of auctions only as an analytical device and not an actual mechanism, it seems likely that the theory requires the working of actual markets as constituents of a just institutional scheme, and that hypothetical markets are not sufficient. The reason for this is that the goods that distributive justice is concerned with should be valued in a way that takes account of the differing ideas of a good life people have, and takes account of them equally. In Dworkin's theory the only way to measure the value of some resource, allocated to one person in a manner that takes an equal account of everyone's interests, is to ask what the actual costs of his/her having that particular resource are for others. This question can be answered only by letting some market mechanism work it out (Dworkin 2000: 66).[10] The market price will reflect the true cost of the asset held by someone to other market actors, providing a standard for an interpersonal comparison of resource holdings that is not biased towards any particular conception of the good life (Dworkin 2000: 70).

If markets do not merely model hypothetical decisions as an analytical device in a theory of justice but are also the only means to measure how certain goods are valued by individuals, in the absence of actual markets, there may be no way for an interpersonal comparison of resource endowments to take place and thus for finding out what requirements follow from Dworkin's egalitarian theory of justice in actual practice. Principles of justice would then be so underdetermined as to be inapplicable because, without existing institutions, we may be unable even to define what a just distribution is. Absent such a definition, principles of justice might not be suitable for assessing alternative distributions or guiding and evaluating individual action and institutional design, in which case they cannot be applied.[11] Thus, existing market institutions constrain the applicability of principles of justice in this theory.[12]

7.5 POLITICAL INSTITUTIONS

We have seen how a specific kind of institutions – markets – can be necessary for making principles of justice determinate by specifying the otherwise indeterminate notion of a fair share of resources. This might be thought an idiosyncrasy of Dworkin's theory which requires a special place for a market pricing mechanism to determine an interpersonally comparable value to distributive shares when goods are heterogeneous and individuals have varying preferences over them. The applicability of these considerations, however, is not unique to Dworkinian theory. The case for a constitutive role of institutions can be generalised to all

theories of distributive justice that include a significant element of procedural justice. To see how institutions play this role, in the remaining
part of the chapter, I focus on political institutions.

I shall assume that political institutions are characterised by the
following features. They possess the capacity to issue and interpret
authoritative rules and decisions for persons within their jurisdiction.
Owing to the coercive powers available to them, they can also enforce
these rules and decisions. Authoritative settlement and enforcement
take place through a public system of law which binds all law subjects
and defines a unique set of rights and obligations for all subjects.[13]

Political institutions play a crucial role in the realisation of principles
of justice. They have an important role to play in filling out the content
of justice by translating abstract principles of justice into specific
rights and obligations for individuals by way of law making and policy
making. In what follows, I outline two considerations supporting this
claim. First, political institutions make the otherwise underdetermined
principles of justice sufficiently determinate by specifying fair distributive shares. Second, they regulate strategic interaction between large
numbers of people whose actions might have an impact on the lives of
numerous others. They are necessary for determining what individuals
ought to do about justice even if fair distributive shares could be determined in the abstract.

7.5.1 *Political institutions specifying fair distributive shares*

We have good reasons to think that, under any plausible conception of
egalitarian justice, fair shares that individuals are entitled to hold are
underdetermined by the principles of justice. Indeterminacy can persist
for various reasons. We already saw one case that concerned the allocation of a given stock of goods among a specific number of individuals.

A second type of indeterminacy about justice in distribution, affecting a much wider range of theories, arises when we introduce a
dynamic perspective into our discussion of distributive justice, taking
into account the need for regulating the social and economic system in
which individuals are to interact. Individuals hold the resources they
are entitled to by justice as their property, which is circumscribed by
public rules. Besides property-law regimes, these public rules circumscribing property include contract and commercial law, laws in criminal
law against force and fraud, public health law, labour regulations and

so on which, together, govern the ownership, production, exchange and use of things. Such rules are necessary for maintaining social cooperation to produce and maintain the resources that individuals need. They affect distributive shares by influencing what goods get produced through social cooperation and how they are distributed. These rules governing property are vague, however, and hence represent another source of otherwise inescapable indeterminacy that institutions can overcome.[14] To take an example, the rule that any transfer of property through sale that was made under duress is void would be incorporated into any plausible conception of what counts as just transfer of property. The term 'under duress', however, is inescapably vague and open to conflicting interpretations. In abstraction from existing institutions, the rule cannot have sufficient specificity that would allow us to apply it to a range of cases. Consequently, we would not be in the position to give a full specification of what our fair shares of resources are.

The indeterminacy of lower-order rules governing the ownership and use of things infects the principles of justice with an element of indeterminacy that we cannot individually overcome.[15] To do this, we need political institutions that can prescribe an authoritative interpretation of such terms which is, to an extent, an arbitrary fact about the rules or directives of institutions. Again, our fair shares of resources are substantially underdetermined because a just distribution cannot be determined independently from just institutions.[16]

Yet another reason for substantive indeterminacy may be found in theories of justice that specify a range of permissible outcomes in distributive matters rather than a unique point. Rawls's theory is indeterminate in this way, too, in at least two of its elements: the rate of just saving required by the theory: and the weight of self-respect in the index of primary goods.[17] Rawls argues that justice requires that we collectively save a sufficient measure of natural and social resources for the benefit of future generations, and that individual self-respect is given proper weight in the distribution of social primary goods. Rawls's principles of justice, however, do not tell us precisely what the just rate of saving should be, nor do they specify how we should weigh self-respect against other primary goods. Instead, they circumscribe a range of permissible values. The values occupying the permissible range entail mutually exclusive arrangements of rules and policies. Society must coordinate on exactly one of these arrangements; such coordination, however, cannot take place through decentralised voluntary agreements owing to the large-scale nature of the setting. Authoritative institutions are necessary to carry out successful co-ordination. If it is a range of outcomes and corresponding rules which is marked out by principles of justice as permissible, then political institutions are to make an authoritative determination of which point within the range society must pursue. Here, too, fair shares of resources are partially determined by the rules or directives of political institutions; thus, there would be no way of knowing them and meeting the requirements of justice prior to, and independently from, these institutions.

7.5.2 *Political institutions governing strategic interaction between individuals*

We have seen why political institutions are indispensable for determining the content of justice in cases when fair individual shares of resources could not, even in principle, be determined independently from, and prior to, their operation. I now turn to a second reason why political institutions determine the content of justice. This consideration, however, applies even to cases when fair individual shares of resources could be determined without institutions. It focuses on the role of the institutions of the basic structure in regulating strategic interaction among individuals, and emphasises the collective nature of various moral requirements, and especially that of requirements of justice.

Moral agency is strategic. The outcome and moral evaluation of our actions are often conditional on the actions of others. For this reason, when making a decision about how to act, we have to take into account the likely actions of others, which we do not control, as a background for our choice. What actions others will take, however, is, in turn, a function of our own action. As a consequence of this strategic feature, there is often no way to determine which course of action one ought to take because there is no information that would be available about the likely actions of others, taken in isolation from one's own future action. In such cases, when individual decisions about moral action are inescapably strategic, coordination is needed among individuals to single out one specific set of actions, indicating that other agents will act in certain ways. Institutional rules are an effective means to perform the requisite coordination; thus, they enable individuals to achieve a morally required or permissible outcome when this is possible only if everyone in a group, or a sufficiently large number of people, follow the same course of action (Waldron 2003: 50).

In addition to necessitating concerted action, moral requirements are often subject to pervasive disagreement. This creates an additional assurance problem because there will be no guarantee that others adhere to a decision about a joint course of action, were such a decision to take place. In cases when individuals have to act in concert, but nevertheless disagree about the morally best joint action, resolution and enforcement are required. By yielding and enforcing authoritative decisions, political institutions can supply assurance to individuals subject to them, and hence of resolve conflicts. Correspondingly, parties are morally required to comply with institutional rules or directives even if they judge some alternative course of action morally superior.[18]

Principles of distributive justice encounter the same problems and thus call for institutional settlement. Suppose again we accept a broadly egalitarian conception of justice which aims to limit the range of socio-economic inequalities among individuals. Egalitarian distributive principles can be realised in more than one way, however, even when we can determine fair distributive shares *ex ante*. The importance of justice being done nonetheless requires that individuals act in a concerted manner and have grounds for forming reasonable expectations about the actions of others involving large stakes. Furthermore, they need assurance that their reasonable expectations are going to be met. To illustrate, I now briefly introduce two problems concerning distributive justice that call for institutional settlement.

One reason why justice requires institutional settlement is that social and economic systems are made up of a number of interrelated institutions and policies, such as property regulations, welfare provisions, educational and health care systems, among others. These constituents admit of several possible combinations that can generate the same distributive outcome. Thus, there might be several combinations of institutions and policies, corresponding to sets of actions, that are equally acceptable under our conception of justice. In such cases, one particular combination must be singled out on what are essentially arbitrary grounds.[19] Political institutions specify the underdetermined demands of egalitarian justice by setting a unique set of distributive rules.

Suppose next that, even though the specific circumstances of the society determine a unique optimally egalitarian institutional scheme, there is disagreement about what this is, given various possible schemes. There are two schemes under consideration, both of which are likely to yield a reasonably just distribution in the society. Scheme A would rely more heavily on a progressive income tax and would keep taxes on consumption low, whereas scheme B would operate with higher consumption taxes and would tax incomes less heavily. Some people think it is scheme A that best serves justice, others think it is scheme B. Governments authoritatively settle debates about distributive justice, and they apply and enforce these decisions on their subjects. By doing so, they determine a unique set of rules and provide assurance that they will be adhered to. Using their effective coercive powers, they will enforce laws even on those subjects who disagree with these. Given that both schemes are reasonably just and that one of them, A, is enacted as law, in the face of a need for coordination and conflict resolution, justice requires one to comply with the rules of A, regardless of whether one thinks it is the best possible egalitarian scheme. This holds even for those subjects who are correct in their judgement that an alternative scheme would be preferable if others followed suit.[20] Thus, political institutions determine what individuals ought to do with regard to justice because of disagreement and the need for conflict resolution in a society.[21]

In both cases, without institutional settlement it would be impossible to tell what justice requires us to do.[22] Institutions are necessary for determining the content of justice even in cases when fair individual shares of resources could, in principle, be determined without institutions.

The political institutions of the basic structure can fill out the content of principles of justice owing to the powers they possess. They coordinate the conduct of individuals and supply assurance by providing authoritative settlement and enforcement through a public system of law which binds all their law subjects. The legal system defines a unique set of rights and obligations for all subjects, backed up by the capacity of political institutions to enforce authoritative rules and decisions within their territory.

7.6 THE SIGNIFICANCE AND PERVASIVENESS OF INDETERMINACY ABOUT JUSTICE

I have argued that basic political and economic institutions play a special role in justice because of a number of indeterminacies in the content of principles. In the absence of existing institutions, the content of distributive principles is substantially underdetermined. The information contained in the principles, together with information about principles of social theory, general economic and social facts, and information about individual preferences and resources available for distribution, are sometimes insufficient to determine what fair shares individuals are entitled to and what actions they ought to undertake in accordance with the principles of justice.[23] Underdetermined principles, however, must be specified before they can guide action and institutional design.

Institutions of the basic structure can specify the underdetermined principles of justice. They determine fair resource shares by singling out a unique set of distributive rules and by enabling an interpersonal comparison of resource holdings. They also define a unique set of rights and obligations for all law subjects that are sufficiently determinate to guide their conduct.

Therefore, I take the political and economic institutions of the basic structure as playing a constitutive role in determining the content of principles of justice. This contrasts with the alternative view I sketched earlier which regards institutions as the most effective means for discharging principles of justice applying prior to, and independently of, the working of these institutions. The view defended in this chapter does not deny that institutions often provide more effective means for bringing about a just distribution and discharging justice-based requirements but it denies that it is all there is to them. It is not the case that institutions merely make independently existing information about fair distributive shares accessible for individuals who, because of individual limitations, cannot themselves gather and process it. Institutions play a constitutive role in determining the content of principles of justice by marking out a unique set of just distributive rules, coordinating individual conduct and providing assurance in cases of disagreement about justice. They make the otherwise indeterminate requirements of justice sufficiently determinate by subjecting individual judgement to rules or directives.

How pervasive is the indeterminacy of principles of justice? The cases discussed earlier show that the requirement of institutional settlement is likely to be a necessary feature of any plausible egalitarian theory of justice. Both disagreement about the demands of justice and the indeterminacy of their content are permanent characteristics of politics.

As for disagreement, John Rawls plausibly argues that a diversity of conflicting views about what is right and good is 'not a mere historical condition that may soon pass away; it is a permanent feature of the public culture of democracy' (Rawls 1999c: 474). Reasonable pluralism, Rawls claims, results from 'the work of free practical reason within the framework of free institutions' (Rawls 1993a: 37). Moral concepts, including the concept of justice, involve various 'burdens of judgment' which make disagreement a permanent feature of life even under free institutions.[24] Also, the complexities of contemporary social life render the demands of egalitarian justice indeterminate. Principles of justice depend for their application on large-scale social coordination, including rules circumscribing property and political processes specifying a unique set of institutions and policies. So, it is in the framework of the basic structure that we make claims of justice because its institutions make the demands of justice determinate for us and resolve disagreement about the right principles and their application.

This function of the basic structure also illuminates the import of the distinction Rawls draws between an institution as an abstract object, that is, as 'a possible form of conduct expressed by a system of rules', and an institution as an actual practice, that is, the way these rules are realised 'in the thought and conduct of certain persons at a certain time and place', when he claims his principles apply to the latter (Rawls 1999a: 48). The foregoing arguments provide one rationale for holding that, even though there may be several possible configurations of the basic structure considered as an abstract object, the principles of justice can sometimes apply only in the context of institutions realised in the conduct of individuals composing them because of the indeterminacy of these principles and the strategic character of the interaction between individuals upholding the institutional scheme.

7.7 THE INDETERMINACY AND APPLICATION OF PRINCIPLES OF JUSTICE

Political and economic institutions are indispensable for specifying the content of principles of distributive justice. Therefore, in the absence of existing institutions, principles of distributive justice might not be applicable, for the reason that these principles are not determinate enough for assessing alternative distributive shares and, even when they could do so, they are not determinate enough for guiding individual conduct. They do not allow judgements about the justice or injustice of some distributions, actions or institutions.

We should consider two potential objections to this argument, both of which would rely on arguments advanced by G. A. Cohen in other contexts. First, Cohen argues that fundamental principles of justice do not depend on facts. Thus, facts of indeterminacy and disagreement, as well as the need for coordination and assurance, are irrelevant for determining the content of fundamental principles of justice. These considerations might be relevant for justifying rules of regulation to govern interaction among agents but they have no bearing on what fundamental principles of justice *are*. Cohen would thus be content with underdetermined principles of justice because he thinks it is not necessarily part of their job to guide action or institutional design.[25] In response to this objection, I have two replies to make. First, I hope to have shown that the content of egalitarian principles of justice is substantially underdetermined, and we might not even be able to tell what *equality* itself – as distinct from other values – consists in without the operation of institutions. Second, however, whatever we think of Cohen's claim about the content of justice, it does not defeat my claim that principles of justice may not *apply* in the absence of institutions, if the application of principles requires that they are capable of evaluating distributions, guiding action or institutional design. It may be true that principles of some sort exist in the absence of institutions but they may not be applied to any site under certain circumstances. The claim this chapter makes is limited to the application of principles of justice; thus, unless one is willing to grant that principles apply even when they cannot possibly assess distributions, guide action or institutional design, the main thesis is not undermined by Cohen's point.

One could further object, however, that the conclusion about the limited applicability of principles of justice is too strong. The indeterminacy of principles, the objection would run, does not preclude making at least some judgements about the justice or injustice of distributions, actions, or institutions. Surely, we do not need working markets or political institutions to see that a world which contains billionaires as well as people below the poverty line is by any egalitarian standard unjust. Because we can make judgements about such flagrant injustices even in the absence of institutions, the objector would conclude, principles of justice do apply in the absence of institutions even when they are indeterminate.[26]

In response to this objection, I should emphasise that the thesis of this chapter is limited in the following sense. The foregoing argument established only that some principles of justice, under some circumstances, fail to be applicable in the absence of institutions. I was not defending the implausibly strong claim that *no* principles of justice ever apply without institutional specification. This chapter shows that, under some circumstances, principles of justice are insufficiently specific to guide individual action or institutional design, or to evaluate distributions; therefore, they cannot be applied to adjudicate distributive questions *under these circumstances*. Take the case when principles of justice specify a range of permissible distributive outcomes rather than a unique point: we know even in the absence of institutions that values lying outside this range are unjust. When we have to decide about the justice or injustice of a distribution within the permissible range, however, principles of justice do not yield a sufficiently determinate answer in the absence of working institutions. I contend that, in such circumstances, for such values, these principles of justice are not applicable. That is, they cannot guide us in evaluating whether any such distribution is unjust, and they cannot guide action and institutional design with regard to these.

7.8 THE SCOPE OF JUSTICE *V.* THE SCOPE OF PRINCIPLES OF JUSTICE

An implication of the constitutive view of the basic structure defended here is that the scope of application of these principles is conditioned by existing institutions. Does this leave us with a relational view of justice? It might seem so for the following reason. We just saw that, to overcome the essential indeterminacy of the content of justice and to coordinate the actions of a large number of individuals, we need political institutions that can issue and enforce authoritative rules and decisions. This capacity is predicated on the coercive force political institutions exercise over their subjects, that is, all those within their territory. It might seem that this commits us to a relational conception of justice along the lines of the arguments of Thomas Nagel and Michael Blake who hold that requirements of distributive justice arise only within the confines of coercively enforced schemes of political institutions (Nagel 2005; Blake 2001). The existence of a certain type of relation, that of being subject to a common set of political and economic institutions, may, after all, be necessary for principles of justice to be applicable to specific distributive problems.[27]

It would be a mistake to equate these two views of political institutions, however. Coercive political institutions enter the two theories at different levels. Relational theories, such as Blake's and Nagel's, regard joint membership in existing institutions as a necessary condition for any kind of justice requirement to arise.[28] There would be no occasion for justice in their absence. The view I am defending, however, is compatible with holding that some requirements of justice can exist independently from, and prior to, coercive political institutions. To take one example, the requirement to promote the establishment of just relations can exist even in the absence of institutions.[29]

To relate this discussion to a term I introduced earlier, the basic structure is not viewed here as foundational in grounding justice. Justice is not grounded in existing institutional relations, even though the application of principles of justice is conditioned by these. The position I defend in the chapter occupies an intermediate ground between those who claim that institutions play a foundational role in the emergence of the requirement to promote justice and those who argue that institutions are mere devices for more effectively carrying out what justice requires us to do anyway.

One qualification is in order at this point. The non-relational theory I started out with assumes that some kind of requirements with regard to justice exists independently of, and prior to, the existence of institutional relations. What this background position implies for cases where common political and economic institutions are non-existent is that everyone has a duty to work towards establishing them so that justice can obtain. The function of political and economic institutions in determining the content of justice I have defended in this chapter, however, is neutral with regard to the ground of justice. The arguments I presented are applicable to relational and to non-relational theories; thus, the two distinctions cut across each other. If, for reasons independent of the considerations I have outlined, we can show that justice is grounded in practice-mediated relations, political and economic institutions still play a constitutive role in defining principles of justice.[30] My arguments do not, however, imply a relational view of institutions.

It might be suggested, however, that the way this theory treats the scope of justice would nevertheless be extensionally equivalent to relational theories. Political institutions can limit the scope of justice because of the role they play in its implementation. They delimit the application of principles of justice and therefore they condition the scope of distributive requirements. In the absence of global political institutions relevantly similar to nation-states, principles of justice may not apply to global distributive questions. The currently existing international mechanisms for enforcing rules, policies and decisions might not be capable of coordinating across the globe and providing assurance that international norms will be effectively enforced. This would make it unlikely that egalitarian distributive principles can be implemented in the international domain.

The reliance, however, of principles of justice on economic and political institutions for their application does not pre-empt the existence of substantial international distributive requirements in the long run even when currently there are no such institutions in place. The obstacles to implementing principles of justice globally are not fixed and can gradually be removed.[31] Even if currently there may not be political institutions at the global level that can perform the same functions as nation-states – most importantly that of making and enforcing authoritative norms – such institutions can evolve in the future. If they could, our duty of justice should guide institutional reform at the global level so that just global institutions can be created.

7.9 THE NATION-STATE SYSTEM AND GLOBAL JUSTICE

Where does this leave us? Do we have to conclude that territorial states are to remain the loci of justice, circumscribing the potential scope of application of principles of justice for the foreseeable future?

This is not very likely. The system of territorial states which has characterised world politics since the Peace of Westphalia in 1648 is undergoing profound changes that provide new opportunities for extending the application of principles of justice to the global domain. Traditionally, the state system has been characterised by the features of territorial sovereignty. States have been exercising political authority over a fixed territorial space. Furthermore, their authority has been regarded as final and exclusive: states have the final say in regulating issues within their territory and no entity within or outside the state's territory has higher authority (Spruyt 1994: 35, 40; Caney 2005: 149–50).[32] The global institutional set-up, however, has gone through a considerable transformation which altered the normative landscape in global politics. Responding to a growing demand for supranational co-ordination and to human rights concerns, territorial political authority has, in practice, been supplemented by a system of global governance. The result is a complex global, multilayered scheme of institutions performing supra- and transnational, regional, and local governance with a mixture of functionally and territorially defined authority. In performing their governance functions, its constituents are at least potentially capable of specifying the content of justice, and thus of enabling the application of principles of justice on global scale. They authoritatively set, interpret and enforce rules worldwide, contributing to the determination of distributive shares and requirements.[33]

Once we accept its global scope, the duty of justice requires that we rely on some of the existing elements of this scheme, reform others so that they better fit principles of justice, and establish new ones, rather than return to the system of territorially defined nation-states.

7.10 SUMMARY AND CONCLUSION

Justice is an institutional virtue in several respects. The debate between relational and non-relational theories concerns whether institutions of the basic structure are necessary for giving rise to requirements of justice and, if so, how they constrain the scope of justice. Thus, the typical strategy pursued by statist theories has been to limit the scope of application of principles of justice by arguing for the foundational role of the basic structure in grounding considerations of justice and pointing out the absence of basic structure at the global level. In this chapter I contrasted this debate about the ground of justice with a different way the basic structure can affect the scope of application of principles of justice. I showed how the basic structure's role in determining the content of justice can affect the scope of application of principles of justice even if we embrace a non-relational cosmopolitan theory. I did so by presenting some considerations that make economic and political institutions indispensable for the realisation of principles of justice. I considered two ways institutions may be partly constitutive of the content of principles of justice. First, I argued that fair distributive shares are substantially underdetermined, and that economic and political institutions are necessary to make them determinate. Economic markets may be required for specifying the value of resources to be distributed. Political institutions are necessary for selecting a unique value from among a range of permissible options, and they also determine fair distributive shares by specifying property. Second, I noted that, even if fair shares of resources could in principle be determined without institutions, there is still a residual indeterminacy about what this implies for individual conduct because of the strategic feature of human action and disagreement about the correct interpretation of principles of justice. I argued that we need political institutions to coordinate individual conduct and provide assurance by making and enforcing authoritative decisions. These considerations showed that, even if we take a non-relational view of justice, political and economic institutions play a constitutive role in determining the content of principles. Fundamental principles of justice themselves do not give a complete specification of what shares of resources individuals are entitled to and what individuals ought to do with regard to justice. Thus, existing institutions may constrain the scope of application of principles of justice because these are not specific enough to guide individual action and institutional design in the abstract. In the absence of the institutions of the basic structure, they may not apply to arising distributive questions. I concluded, however, by arguing that existing nation-states do not represent the outer bounds of justice because the global institutional set-up can be reformed so as to become more sensitive to the demands of global justice.

Notes

1 This chapter is an adapted version of my previous article, 'The Basic Structure and the Principles of Justice', *Utilitas*, volume 23, issue 2, 2011, pp. 161–82. Copyright © Cambridge University Press 2011. Reprinted with permission.

2 Recall that Rawls defines the basic structure of society as 'the way in which the major social institutions distribute fundamental rights and duties and determine the division of advantages from social cooperation' (Rawls, 1999a, p. 6).

3 This is how Rawls describes the constituents of the basic structure. This structure includes, among other things, laws governing income and property taxation, fiscal and economic policy (Rawls, 1999a, p. 6; Rawls, 1993a, pp. 258, 282–3.

4 See the discussion by Abizadeh (2007).

5 In the article on which this chapter is based, I claimed that non-relational

theories are necessarily cosmopolitan (Miklós, 2011). This is not so, however. Non-relational non-cosmopolitan theories are conceivable because the scope of justice can be limited by conditions other than membership in special relations. For example, we may think that justice holds only between persons with blue eyes. Nonetheless, all non-relational theories that have actually been advocated are cosmopolitan, including those that I discussed in Chapter 6.

6 It is important to remember from our earlier discussion that non-relational theories are only a subset of cosmopolitan theories. There are relational cosmopolitan theories too. First of all, we might be statists or cosmopolitans, depending on *what kind* of relation we regard as foundational for grounding justice. For example, Nagel's political conception of justice – a statist theory – can be contrasted here with globalised Rawlsianism – a cosmopolitan relational view. On the other hand, disagreement about the scope of justice need not represent a disagreement about the ground of justice, either between non-relational and relational views, or between different versions of relational theories. Relational cosmopolitans and statists may agree on the proper ground of justice and still disagree about the scope of its application because of disagreement about the empirical question whether or not the requisite relation holds globally. Recall cosmopolitan and statist interpretations of Rawlsian theory. I shall discuss how the argument bears on relational theories later in this chapter.

7 In this chapter I aim to remain neutral among competing conceptions of egalitarian justice with regard to both the currency of justice and specific distributive principles insofar as they aim to reduce socio-economic inequalities. Much of its argument holds for both resourcist and welfarist theories of distributive justice though one argument relies on Dworkin's specific resourcist version.

8 This premise is not uncontroversial. As we shall see later, G. A. Cohen rejects the claim that fundamental principles of justice should be able to guide action. I shall consider Cohen's position in a later section. On the other hand, the stated premise is deliberately vague about the sites to which principles of justice can apply. By referring to the capacity of principles to assess states of affairs or to guide individual conduct and/or institutional design, I mean to leave open the question of whether principles of justice apply to only one of these sites or to several of them.

9 Saladin Meckled-Garcia further elaborates this point in Meckled-Garcia, 2008: 256–9.

10 One consideration motivating this thought is Dworkin's reliance on a 'norm of liberty', requiring that measurement should be made on the assumption – to the extent this is possible – 'that others would have been

free to use the resources in question as they wished if these were theirs instead' (Dworkin, 2000, p. 183).

11 David Miller suggests this point about Dworkin's theory. On the basis of this, he goes on to argue against global requirements of justice; as we shall see, however, this conclusion does not follow. For his argument see Miller, 1999.

12 This is so even if markets need to be supplemented with redistributive policies. Dworkin thinks justice requires this because the theory needs to account for differential natural endowments – talents and handicaps – as well.

13 See the accounts by David Copp (1999) and A. John Simmons (2001).

14 By the vagueness of these rules I mean the fact that they admit of a significant range of borderline cases where the application of the rule is unclear and subject to disagreement.

15 It might be asked, is it not possible to perfect these rules until they are precise enough to overcome indeterminacy? No, because, as Timothy Endicott persuasively argues in the context of the vagueness of law, the use of vague evaluative standards such as 'dangerous', 'careless', or 'reasonable', and descriptive terms such as 'income' (for the purpose of determining the tax base) is necessary in order to be able to regulate a wide range of human activities while still being able to serve as a guide for the conduct of individual citizens and officials (Endicott, 2001, pp. 379–85. For a classic account of the vagueness of law, see Hart, 1994, pp. 124–36.

16 This indeterminacy can take two basic forms. First, we can hold with Hume that property rights are entirely conventional, in which case there is no way to give even an approximate account of a just property regime in the absence of relevant conventions. Institutions, insofar as they provide us with the requisite conventions, fill out the content of justice by specifying a determinate set of property rights. Second, we might hold with Locke that some kinds of natural property rights exist that can be defined in abstraction from existing institutions. As Locke himself recognises, however, even in this case we would have to face indeterminacy about the interpretation of such rights at the margins, which can be overcome only with the help of institutions capable of providing an authoritative settlement (Hume, 1976, p. 489; Locke, 1988, pp. 350–1, 358–9).

17 Rawls acknowledges this indeterminacy in Rawls, 1999a, pp. 176, 318.

18 See the general argument for the value of democracy along these lines in Jeremy Waldron (1999b). For an illuminating account of the moral significance of political institutions see János Kis (2008).

19 For an elaboration of this point with a focus on political obligation, see Waldron, 1993, p. 24.

20 Here I have in mind what Rawls calls a situation of near justice where

principles of justice are more or less satisfied by the regime (Rawls, 1999a, p. 310).

21 It might be objected that, by making reference to the need for assurance in the face of disagreement, I introduce considerations extraneous to justice. Such considerations might be important in their own right, the objection would run. They are, however, immaterial for determining what justice consists in. This claim is very implausible, however. Rawls divides his theory of justice to ideal and non-ideal theory. Ideal theory deals with circumstances when everybody complies strictly with principles of justice and when circumstances are favourable for a just society. My argument shows that, even if we can define the collectively optimal *ideally* just scheme independently of assurance considerations, these considerations are relevant for evaluating alternative courses of action or states of affairs in non-ideal circumstances. Given the *actual* conduct of others, justice can be better approximated if one complies with scheme A rather than trying to follow any other scheme. Thus, unless one holds the implausible position that justice does not favour courses of action which better approximate ideal justice than alternative courses would, one has to accept that assurance considerations do affect justice.

22 In the disagreement case, we can know the collectively optimal ideal scheme. We do not know, however, if one's individual actions that would be in line with this scheme are indeed what justice requires, given the actual conduct of others.

23 It is worth emphasising here that the argument in this chapter does not turn on the lack of public verifiability of compliance with principles. The argument established not only that sometimes we cannot tell whether other individuals comply with principles of justice but it also showed why in some circumstances it is impossible to know what justice requires even *in foro interno*. For an argument against the publicity criterion for principles of justice, attacking the verifiability requirement, see Cohen, 2008, pp. 349–54.

24 For an explanation of why this is so see Rawls, 1993a, pp. 54–8.

25 For Cohen's position see Cohen, 2008, especially Chapters 6–8.

26 G. A. Cohen mounts this criticism against Andrew Williams's argument from publicity (Cohen, 2008, Chapter 8, section 5).

27 Analogous considerations apply to the role of economic institutions in partially constituting principles of justice by defining fair shares of resources. Principles of justice may not be applicable among individuals who do not stand in the relation of being market actors in the same market.

28 The same could be said about Andrea Sangiovanni's 'practice-dependence thesis', if the latter is taken to mean that institutions are necessary for the

existence of requirements of justice. Unlike Nagel and Blake, and similarly to my account, Sangiovanni emphasises the manner institutions may be necessary to make precise the underdetermined content of justice. Sangiovanni seems to conclude, however, that this function makes institutions necessary for the existence of 'first principles of justice', which claim is not entailed by my position (Sangiovanni, 2008, pp. 138–9).

29 Here I refer to what Rawls calls our natural duty of justice. An important feature of the natural duty of justice is that it is pre-institutional. For Rawls, this means the conjunction of two things: such duties apply to individuals regardless of their voluntary acts; and they apply to them prior to, and independently of, the rules of institutions. As Rawls puts it, the content of such duties 'is not, in general, defined by the rules of [institutions]' (Rawls, 1999a, p. 98).

30 Note that we can make the central argument of the chapter in a relational context. In this case, justice would be restricted to those individuals who stand in some special relationship, say to those who are fellow citizens of a state, or to those subject to a common set of institutions. This is compatible with saying that the roles institutions play in grounding requirements of justice and in defining them are distinct.

31 Arash Abizadeh argues that, even if no just global basic structure is feasible, the scope of justice is still global. He claims that, even if justice cannot be fully attained, it can be realised to greater or lesser degrees; hence, justice directs us to employ the instruments capable of realising it to a greater degree (Abizadeh, 2007, pp. 340–1). My argument implies, however, that, without a basic structure, it may not be possible to see what greater or lesser justice would consist in and, even if it can, it might not be possible to know how to go about realising it.

32 When they claim political authority, territorial states do not merely assert the fact of their actual power over a number of people or over a territory. What they claim are various rights. They claim the right to be the exclusive imposer and enforcer of legal requirements on people within their territory. They also claim rights against aliens to be immune from their interference with exercising their authority over their subjects and territory, and also to control and prohibit movement across their border. Finally, they claim rights over regulating the use of their territory. For a typology of these rights see Copp, 1999; Simmons, 2001. For an account of the rights of states focusing on public health see Miklós, 2009b.

33 As discussed earlier, Joshua Cohen and Charles Sabel convincingly argue that globalisation has created a normatively relevant set of global institutions of an intermediate type. They show that, in many areas of regulation, the making, interpretation and application of rules take place 'in global settings' that perform these functions 'with some de facto decision making

independence from their creators' (i.e., states). As a consequence, 'there is a direct rule-making relationship between global bodies and the citizens of different states', in which these global bodies impose and enforce rules on individuals worldwide (Cohen and Sabel 2006, pp. 165–75). Even though Cohen and Sabel focus on the normative role of these structures in generating global distributive requirements, my argument showed how institutional schemes conducting these governance functions can play a different sort of normative role, namely that of enabling the application of principles of justice by specifying them.

CONCLUSION

Global socio-economic inequalities raise important philosophical questions about justice. Are dramatic global inequalities in life prospects unjust, giving residents of affluent countries reasons to reduce them beyond their humanitarian obligations to mitigate suffering and prevent easily preventable deaths? If so, what considerations are these duties of justice based on? Can we apply globally the principles of justice that we accept for the domestic domain? In this book, I have shown that focusing on institutions is helpful for answering these questions.

In particular, to determine whether special relationships that institutions represent are normatively significant, I have analysed the roles that social, economic and political institutions play in conditioning the justification, the scope and the content of principles of distributive justice. I have shown that different understandings of the normative significance of institutions motivate much of the current disagreement about whether or not requirements of justice have a global scope. More specifically, I have described two different normative functions that institutions may have in theories of justice. First, I critically evaluated a number of positions about the role of institutions in generating requirements of distributive justice, and considered their implications for the scope of justice. Second, I defended a position about the role political and economic institutions play in determining the content of requirements of distributive justice, and I showed how they can affect the scope of application of these requirements.

I have distinguished three questions about justice that need to be addressed. First, what is the scope of justice, that is, what is the range of persons who have responsibilities to one another arising from considerations of justice? Second, are special relations, such as institutions, necessary for the existence of requirements of justice? Third, how do institutions relate to the content of justice? While discussing these questions, I took distributive justice to concern particularly stringent claims over absolute or relative shares of things that are generally regarded valuable, such as rights to income and wealth. These claims concern entitlements to distributive shares rather than duties of beneficence, charity or humanity.

With regard to the scope of justice, I have distinguished cosmopolitan and statist positions. Whereas cosmopolitans hold that principles of justice include every human being within their scope, statists argue that the scope of justice is limited to fellow citizens in the same state. Statists deny that we have obligations of distributive justice to foreigners though they allow for other, more limited, moral obligations to them: we are required to respect the basic human rights of people in less developed countries; to provide humanitarian assistance to alleviate poverty and suffering; and to rescue the poorest from hunger-related death. I have addressed the debate between cosmopolitans and statists by considering the ground of justice, evaluating morally relevant features that may be necessary to give rise to requirements of justice. I described various relational conceptions of justice that regard practice-mediated relations as necessary for the existence of requirements of justice, and also some non-relational arguments that deny this. I considered the implications of these theories for the scope of justice. I have defended a cosmopolitan conception of distributive justice, in which the scope of justice is not limited to nation-states, by arguing against statist positions that limit the scope of distributive justice to national political communities on the basis of various relational conceptions of justice. The relational theories of justice I discussed regard national ties or domestic institutions and policies regulating social and economic inequalities as necessary to generate requirements of distributive justice. These institutions and policies are regarded as foundational insofar as they employ coercive force against their subjects, or authoritatively regulate cooperation among fellow citizens, or have a profound and pervasive effect on individual lives. Responding to these theories, I have argued that these relational theories cannot justify statism. Their most plausible version will yield a relational cosmopolitan conclusion. I have also described non-relational reasons for recognising some requirements of distributive justice outside institutionally governed interaction. I have rehearsed arguments for the claim that distributive requirements can exist on different grounds, such as by virtue of our common humanity or competing claims by agents to scarce natural resources. Global institutions are not necessary to generate global requirements of justice.

Having discussed the role of institutions in generating requirements of distributive justice, I analysed in detail a distinct normative function institutions perform by determining the content of principles of justice. I have distinguished two different conceptions of how institutions can relate to the content of justice. The standard view regards institutions as effective instruments to carry out requirements of justice that apply independently from these institutions, with their content given prior to the rules of any institutions. In contrast with this, I have defended a different view that regards institutions as playing a constitutive role in determining the content of justice. I have argued that political and economic institutions can limit the applicability of principles of justice even in a cosmopolitan conception. In the absence of existing institutions, fundamental principles of justice are not determinate enough for assessing alternative distributive shares and for guiding and evaluating individual conduct and institutional design. Therefore, they cannot be applied with a global scope to adjudicate all distributive issues even in non-relational cosmopolitan egalitarian theories. Political and economic institutions partially constitute the content of justice and enable the application of principles of justice by determining fair distributive shares and by resolving indeterminacies about justice-based requirements resulting from strategic interaction and disagreement. This view of institutions is not a relational conception of justice, however, because it is compatible with holding that some requirements of justice can exist independently from, and prior to, coercive political institutions.

The book has achieved two goals. First, assuming that egalitarian requirements of distributive justice are part of an attractive position about domestic justice, it has shown that there are compelling reasons to accept such requirements for the global domain. Second, it has developed a novel theory about a normative function institutions perform in the application of requirements of cosmopolitan justice. Besides their instrumental role in implementing pre-institutional distributive requirements, institutions play a constitutive role in determining the content of requirements of distributive justice.

BIBLIOGRAPHY

Abizadeh, Arash (2007), 'Cooperation, Pervasive Impact, and Coercion: on the Scope (not Site) of Distributive Justice', *Philosophy and Public Affairs*, pp. 318–58.

Anderson, Elizabeth (1999), 'What is the Point of Equality?', *Ethics* 109 (January), pp. 287–337.

Arneson, Richard (1989), 'Equality of Opportunity for Welfare', *Philosophical Studies* 56, pp. 77–93.

Baldwin, Thomas (1992), 'The Territorial State', in H. Gross and R. Harrison (eds), *Jurisprudence: Cambridge Essays* (Oxford: Oxford University Press).

Barry, Brian (1973), *The Liberal Theory of Justice* (Oxford: Oxford University Press).

—(1989), *Theories of Justice: A Treatise on Social Justice*, vol. 1 (Oxford: Clarendon Press).

—(1991), 'Humanity and Justice in a Global Perspective', in *Liberty and Justice* (Oxford: Clarendon Press).

Beitz, Charles R. (1979), *Political Theory and International Relations* (Princeton, NJ: Princeton University Press).

—(1983), 'Cosmopolitan Ideals and National Sentiment', *Journal of Philosophy*, vol. 80, no. 1, pp. 591–600.

—(1994), 'Cosmopolitan Liberalism and the States System', in Chris Brown (ed.), *Political Restructuring in Europe* (London: Routledge).

—(1999a), *Political Theory and International Relations* 2nd ed. (Princeton, NJ: Princeton University Press).

—(1999b), 'Social and Cosmopolitan Liberalism', *International Affairs*, vol. 75, no. 3, pp. 515–29.

—(1999c), 'International Liberalism and Distributive Justice: A Survey of Recent Thought', *World Politics* 51, pp. 697–721.

—(2000), 'Rawls's Law of Peoples', *Ethics* 110, July 2000, pp. 669–96.

—(2001), 'Does Global Inequality Matter?', in Thomas W. Pogge (ed.), *Global Justice* (Oxford: Blackwell).

Blake, Michael (2001), 'Distributive Justice, State Coercion, and Autonomy', *Philosophy and Public Affairs*, vol. 30, no. 3, July 2001, pp. 257–96.

Brown, Eric and Kleingeld, Pauline (2002), 'Cosmopolitanism', in *Stanford Encyclopedia of Philosophy*. Available at http.//plato.stanford.edu/entries/cosmospolitanism.

Buchanan, Allen (2000), 'Rawls's Law of Peoples: Rules for a Vanished Westphalian World', *Ethics*, vol. 110, no. 4, pp. 697–721.

—(2003), *Justice, Legitimacy, and Self-Determination* (Oxford: Oxford University Press).

Caney, Simon (2002), 'Cosmopolitanism and the Law of Peoples', *The Journal of Political Philosophy*, vol. 10, pp. 95–123.

—(2005), *Justice Beyond Borders* (Oxford: Oxford University Press).

Chen, Shaohua and Ravallion, Martin (2004), 'How Have the World's Poorest Fared Since the Early 1980s?', *World Bank Research Observer* 19.

Cohen, G. A. (1989), 'On the Currency of Egalitarian Justice', *Ethics* 99, pp. 906–44.

—(2000), 'Political Philosophy and Personal Behavior', in *If You're an Egalitarian, How Come You're So Rich?* (Cambridge, MA: Harvard University Press).

—(2008), *Rescuing Justice and Equality* (Cambridge, MA: Harvard University Press).

Cohen, Joshua (2001), 'Taking People as They Are?', *Philosophy and Public Affairs*, vol. 30, no. 4, pp. 383–6.

Cohen, Joshua and Sabel, Charles (2006), 'Extra Republicam Nulla Justitia?', *Philosophy and Public Affairs* vol. 34, no. 2, pp. 147–75.

Copp, David (1999), 'The Idea of a Legitimate State', *Philosophy and Public Affairs*, vol. 28, no. 1.

Daniels, Norman (2003), 'Democratic Equality: Rawls's Complex Egalitarianism', in Samuel Freeman (ed.), *The Cambridge Companion to Rawls* (Cambridge: Cambridge University Press).

—(2008), *Just Health* (Cambridge, Cambridge University Press).

Diamond, Jared (1999), *Guns, Germs, and Steel: The Fates of Human Societies* (New York: Norton).

Dworkin, Ronald M. (1985), *A Matter of Principle* (Cambridge, MA: Harvard University Press).

—(1986), *Law's Empire* (Cambridge, MA: Harvard University Press).

—(1996), *Freedom's Law: The Moral Reading of the American Constitution* (New York: Oxford University Press).

—(2000), *Sovereign Virtue* (Cambridge, MA: Harvard University Press).

Endicott Timothy (2001), 'Law is Necessarily Vague', *Legal Theory*, vol. 7, no. 4, pp. 379–85.

Eyal, Nir and Hurst, Samia (2008), 'Physician Brain Drain – Can Nothing Be Done?', in *Public Health Ethics* 1, no. 2, pp. 1–13.

Fabre, Cecile (2007), *Justice in a Changing World* (Cambridge: Polity Press).

FAO (United Nations Food and Agriculture Organization) (1999), *The State of Food Insecurity in the World in 1999*. Available at www.fao.org/news/1999/img/sofi-e.pdf

Feinberg, Joel (1980), 'Noncomparative Justice', in *Rights, Justice, and the Bounds of Liberty* (Princeton, NJ: Princeton University Press).

Franck, Thomas M. (1995), *Fairness in International Law and Institutions* (Oxford: Clarendon Press).

Frankfurt, Harry (1988), 'Equality as a Moral Ideal', in *The Importance of What We Care About* (Cambridge: Cambridge University Press).

Freeman, Samuel (2006a), 'The Law of Peoples, Social Cooperation, Human Rights, and Distributive Justice', *Social Philosophy and Policy.*, vol. 23, no. 1, pp. 29–68.

—(2006b), 'Distributive Justice and The Law of Peoples', in Rex Martin and David A. Reidy (eds), *Rawls's Law of Peoples, A Realistic Utopia?*, pp. 243–60 (Oxford: Blackwell).

Goodin, Robert E. (1988), 'What is So Special about Our Fellow Countrymen?' *Ethics*, vol. 98, no. 4, pp. 663–86.

Grotius, Hugo (2005), edited with an Introduction by Richard Tuck, *The Rights of War and Peace* (Indianapolis: Liberty Press).

Hardin, Garrett (1968), 'The Tragedy of the Commons', *Science* 162, pp. 1243–8.

Harman, Gilbert (1989), 'Is There a Single True Morality?', in M. Krausz (ed.), *Relativism: Interpretation and Confrontation*, pp. 363–86 (Notre Dame, IN: University of Notre Dame Press).

Hart, H. L. A. (1955), 'Are There Any Natural Rights?', *Philosophical Review* 64 (2), pp. 175–191.

—(1994), *The Concept of Law* 2nd ed. (Oxford: Oxford University Press).

Hayek, F. A. (1960), *The Constitution of Liberty* (Chicago, IL: University of Chicago Press).

Held, David and McGrew, Anthony (eds) (1999), *Global Transformations* (London: Polity Press).

Hume, David (1740/1976), L. A. Selby-Brigge. (ed.), rev. 3rd ed., P. H. Nidditch (ed.), *A Treatise of Human Nature* (Oxford: Oxford University Press).

Hurka, Thomas (1997), 'The Justification of National Partiality', in Robert McKim and Jeff McMahan (eds), *The Morality of Nationalism* (Oxford: Oxford University Press).

Julius, A. J. (2006), 'Nagel's Atlas', *Philosophy and Public Affairs*, vol. 34, no. 2, pp. 113–47.

Kant, Immanuel (1991), Mary Gregor (ed.) *The Metaphysics of Morals* (Cambridge: Cambridge University Press).

—(1992), 'Perpetual Peace', in Hans Reiss (ed.), *Political Writings* (Cambridge: Cambridge University Press).

Keohane, Robert O. (1984), *After Hegemony* (Princeton, NJ: Princeton University Press).

—(2002), *Power and Governance in a Partially Globalized World* (London: Routledge).

Kis, János (2001), 'Nation-Building and Beyond', in Will Kymlicka and Magda Opalski, *Can Liberal Pluralism Be Exported?* (Oxford: Oxford University Press).

—(2008), *Politics as a Moral Problem* (Budapest: Central European University Press).

Klosko, George (1992), *The Principle of Fairness and Political Obligation* (Oxford: Rowman and Littlefield).

—(2005), *Political Obligations* (Oxford: Oxford University Press).

Kremer, Michael and Glennerster, Rachel (2004), *Strong Medicine: Creating Incentives for Pharmaceutical Research on Neglected Diseases* (Princeton NJ: Princeton University Press).

Kuper, Andrew (2000), 'Rawlsian Global Justice', *Political Theory*, vol. 28, pp. 640–74.

Landes, David S. (1998), *The Wealth and Poverty of Nations* (London: Little, Brown).

Locke, John (1988), Peter Laslett (ed.), *Two Treatises of Government* (Cambridge: Cambridge University Press).

MacIntyre, Alasdair (1985), *After Virtue: A Study in Moral Theory* (London: Duckworth).

Margalit, Avishai and Raz, Joseph (1994), 'On National Self-Determination', in Joseph Raz (ed.) *Ethics in the Public Domain* (Oxford: Oxford University Press).

Meckled-Garcia, Saladin (2008), 'On the Very Idea of Cosmopolitan Justice: Constructivism and International Agency', *Journal of Political Philosophy*, pp. 245–71.

Miklós, András (2009a), 'Nationalist Criticisms of Cosmopolitan Justice', *Public Reason* 1 (1), pp. 105–24.

— (2009b), 'Public Health and the Rights of States', *Public Health Ethics* 2 (2), July 2009, pp. 158–70.

—(2011), 'The Basic Structure and the Principles of Justice', *Utilitas* 23 (2), June 2011, pp. 161–82.

Miller, David (1995), *On Nationality* (Oxford: Clarendon Press).

—(1999), 'Justice and Global Inequality', in Andrew Hurrell and Ngaire Woods (eds), *Inequality, Globalization, and World Politics* (Oxford: Oxford University Press).

—(2005), 'Against Global Egalitarianism', *The Journal of Ethics* (9), pp. 55–79.

—(2007), *National Responsibility and Global Justice* (Oxford: Oxford University Press).

Miller, Richard (1998), 'Cosmopolitan Respect and Patriotic Concern', *Philosophy and Public Affairs* 27, pp. 202–24.

—(2010), *Globalizing Justice* (Oxford: Oxford University Press).

Miller, Seamus (2010), *The Moral Foundations of Social Institutions* (Cambridge: Cambridge University Press).

Moellendorf, Darrel (2002), *Cosmopolitan Justice* (Boulder, CO: Westview Press).

Moore, Margaret (2001), *The Ethics of Nationalism* (Oxford: Oxford University Press).

Mulhall, Stephen and Swift, Adam (1992), *Liberals and Communitarians* (Oxford: Blackwell).

Murphy, Liam B. (1999), 'Institutions and the Demands of Justice', *Philosophy and Public Affairs* 27, no. 4, pp. 251–91.

Nagel, Thomas (1977), 'Poverty and Food: Why Charity is Not Enough', in Peter Brown and Henry Shue (eds) *Food Policy: The Responsibility of the United States in the Life and Death Choices* (New York: The Free Press).

—(2002), 'Justice and Nature', in *Concealment and Exposure* (Oxford: Oxford University Press).

—(2005), 'The Problem of Global Justice', *Philosophy and Public Affairs* 33, no. 2, pp. 113–47.

Nielsen, Kai (1988), 'World Government, Security, and Global Justice', in Steven Luper-Foy (ed.) *Problems of International Justice* (Boulder, CO: Westview Press).

Nozick, Robert (1974), *Anarchy, State, and Utopia* (New York: Basic Books).

Nussbaum, Martha (2000), *Women and Human Development: The Capabilities Approach* (Cambridge: Cambridge University Press).

O'Neill, Onora (1974), 'Lifeboat Earth', *Philosophy and Public Affairs* 4, no. 3, pp. 273–92.

—Onora (2000), *Bounds of Justice* (Cambridge: Cambridge University Press).

Parfit, Derek (1984), *Reasons and Persons* (Oxford: Oxford University Press).

Patten, Alan (2005), 'Should We Stop Thinking about Poverty in Terms of Helping the Poor?', *Ethics and International Affairs* 19, no. 1, pp. 19–27.

Pogge, Thomas W. (1989), *Realizing Rawls* (Ithaca, NY: Cornell University Press).

—(1994), 'An Egalitarian Law of Peoples', *Philosophy and Public Affairs*, vol. 23, no. 3, pp. 195–224.

—(1995), 'Three Problems with Contractarian–Consequentialist Ways of Assessing Social Institutions', *Social Philosophy and Policy*, vol. 12, no. 2, pp. 241–66.

—(2000), 'On the Site of Distributive Justice: Reflections on Cohen and Murphy', *Philosophy and Public Affairs* vol. 29, no. 2, pp. 137–69.

—(2001a), 'Priorities of Global Justice', in Thomas Pogge (ed.), *Global Justice* (Oxford: Blackwell).

—(2001b), 'Rawls on International Justice', *The Philosophical Quarterly* vol. 51, pp. 246–53.

—(2002), *World Poverty and Human Rights* (Cambridge: Polity Press).

—(2005a), 'World Poverty and Human Rights', *Ethics and International Affairs* 19, no. 1, pp. 1–7.

—(2005b), 'Severe Poverty as a Violation of Negative Duties', *Ethics and International Affairs* 19, no. 1, pp. 55–83.

—(2006), 'Do Rawls's Two Theories of Justice Fit Together?', in Rex Martin and David A. Reidy (eds), *Rawls's Law of Peoples* (Oxford: Blackwell).

—(2010), 'The Health Impact Fund: Better Pharmaceutical Innovations at Much Lower Prices', in T. Pogge, M. Rimmer and K. Rubenstein (eds), *Incentives for Global Health: Patent Law and Access to Essential Medicines* (Cambridge: Cambridge University Press).

Ravallion, Martin (2012), 'An Update to the World Bank's Estimates of Consumption Poverty in the Developing World'. Available at http://site resources.worldbank.org/INTPOVCALNET/Resources/Global_Poverty_Up date_2012_02-29-12.pdf, accessed 26 March 2012.

Rawls, John (1971), *A Theory of Justice* (Cambridge, MA: Harvard University Press).

—'Kantian Constructivism in Moral Theory', *Journal of Philosophy* 77.

—(1993a), *Political Liberalism* (New York: Columbia University Press).

—(1993b), 'The Law of Peoples', in Stephen Shute and Susan Hurley (eds), *On Human Rights: The Oxford Amnesty Lectures* (New York: Basic Books).

—(1999a), *A Theory of Justice*, rev. ed. (Cambridge, MA: Harvard University Press).

—(1999b.), *The Law of Peoples* (Cambridge, MA: Harvard University Press).

—(1999c), *Collected Papers* (Cambridge, MA: Harvard University Press).

—(2001), *Justice as Fairness: A Restatement* (Cambridge, MA: Harvard University Press).

Raz, Joseph (1984), 'The Obligation to Obey: Revision and Tradition', *Notre Dame Journal of Law, Ethics and Public Policy.*

—(1986), *The Morality of Freedom* (Oxford: Clarendon Press).

—(1990), *Practical Reasons and Norms*, 2nd ed. (Oxford: Oxford University Press).

Richards, David A. J. (1982), 'International Distributive Justice', in J. R. Pennock and J. W. Chapman (eds), *Ethics, Economics and the Law* (Oxford: Oxford University Press), pp. 275–99.

Risse, Mathias (2005a), 'Do We Owe the Global Poor Assistance or Rectification?', *Ethics and International Affairs*, vol. 19, no. 1, pp. 9–18.

—(2005b), 'What We Owe to the Global Poor', *The Journal of Ethics*, pp. 81–117.

—Mathias (2005c), 'How Does the Global Order Harm the Poor?', *Philosophy and Public Affairs* 33 (4), pp. 350–75.

—(2009), 'Common Ownership of the Earth as a Non-Parochial Standpoint: A Contingent Derivation of Human Rights', *European Journal of Philosophy* 17 (2), pp. 277–304.

Sachs, Jeffrey (2001), 'Tropical Underdevelopment', *National Bureau of Economic Research Working Paper* 8119.

Sandel, Michael J. (1982), *Liberalism and the Limits of Justice* (Cambridge: Cambridge University Press).

Sangiovanni, Andrea (2007), 'Global Justice, Reciprocity, and the State', *Philosophy and Public Affairs*, pp. 3–39.

—(2008), 'Justice and the Priority to Morality', *Journal of Political Philosophy* (16), 2, pp. 137–64.

Satz, Debra (1999), 'Equality of What among Whom?', in Ian Shapiro and Lea Brilmayer (eds), *Global Justice* (New York: New York University Press).

—(2005), 'What Do We Owe the Global Poor?' *Ethics and International Affairs* 19, no. 1, pp. 47–54.

Scanlon, T. M. 1989 (1975). 'Rawls's Theory of Justice', in Norman Daniels (ed.), *Reading Rawls* (Stanford, CA: Stanford University Press).

—(2003), 'The Diversity of Objections to Inequality', in *The Difficulty of Tolerance* (Cambridge: Cambridge University Press).

Scheffler, Samuel (2001), *Boundaries and Allegiances* (Oxford: Oxford University Press).

—(2003a), 'Rawls and Utilitarianism', in Samuel Freeman (ed.), *The Cambridge Companion to Rawls* (Cambridge: Cambridge University Press).

—(2003b), 'What is Egalitarianism?', *Philosophy and Public Affairs*, vol. 31, no. 1, pp. 5–39.

Schmidtz, David (1991), *The Limits of Government* (Boulder, CO: Westview Press).

Segall, Shlomi (2010), *Health, Luck and Justice* (Princeton, NJ: Princeton University Press).

Sen, Amartya (1992), *Inequality Reexamined* (Oxford: Oxford University Press).

Shue, Henry (1996), *Basic Rights: Subsistence, Affluence, and U.S. Foreign Policy*, 2nd ed. (Princeton, NJ: Princeton University Press).

Simmons, A. John (1979), *Moral Principles and Political Obligation* (Princeton, NJ: Princeton University Press).

—(1996), 'Associative Political Obligations', *Ethics* 106.

—(2001), 'On the Territorial Rights of States', in *Philosophical Issues* 11.

Singer, Peter (1972), 'Famine, Affluence, and Morality', *Philosophy and Public Affairs*, vol. 1, no. 3, pp. 229–43.

—(2002), *One World* (New Haven, CT: Yale University Press).

Slaughter, Anne-Marie (2004), *A New World Order* (Princeton, NJ: Princeton University Press).

Spruyt, Hendrik (1994), *The Sovereign State and Its Competitors* (Princeton, NJ: Princeton University Press).

Steiner, Hillel (1994), *An Essay On Rights* (Cambridge: Blackwell).

—(2005), 'Territorial Justice and Global Redistribution', in H. Brighouse and G. Brock (eds), *The Political Philosophy of Cosmopolitanism* (Cambridge: Cambridge University Press).

Tamir, Yael (1995), *Liberal Nationalism* (Princeton NJ: Princeton University Press).

Tan, Kok-Chor (2004), *Justice Without Borders: Cosmopolitanism, Nationalism, and Patriotism* (Cambridge: Cambridge University Press).

Taylor, Charles (1989), *Sources of the Self* (Cambridge, MA: Harvard University Press).

—(1994), 'The Politics of Recognition', in Amy Gutmann (ed.), *Multiculturalism: Examining the Politics of Recognition* (Princeton, NJ: Princeton University Press).

Teson, Fernando (1995), 'The Rawlsian Theory of International Law', *Ethics and International Affairs*, vol. 9, no. 1, pp. 79–99.

UNDP (United Nations Development Programme) (1996), *Human Development Report 1996* (Oxford: Oxford University Press).

—(2004), *Human Development Report 2004* (New York: UNDP).

Unger, Peter (1996), *Living High and Letting Die: Our Illusion of Innocence* (Oxford: Oxford University Press).

UNICEF (United Nations Children's Fund) (2005), *The State of the World's Children 2005* (New York: UNICEF).

—(2006), *The State of the World's Children 2006* (New York: UNICEF).

Waldron, Jeremy (1993), 'Special Ties and Natural Duties', *Philosophy and Public Affairs*, vol. 22, no. 1, pp. 3–30.

—(1995), 'Money and Complex Equality', in David Miller and Michael Walzer (eds), *Pluralism, Justice, and Equality* (Oxford: Oxford University Press).

—(1999a), *The Dignity of Legislation* (Cambridge: Cambridge University Press).

—(1999b), *Law and Disagreement* (Oxford: Oxford University Press).

—(2000), 'What is Cosmopolitan?', *Journal of Political Philosophy*, vol. 8, no. 2, pp. 227–43.

—(2003), 'Authority for Officials', in Lukas H. Meyer, Stanley L. Paulson, and Thomas W. Pogge (eds), *Rights, Culture, and the Law* (Oxford: Oxford University Press).

Walzer, Michael (1983), *Spheres of Justice* (New York: Basic Books).

Wenar, Leif (2002), 'The Legitimacy of Peoples', in Ciaran Cronin and Pablo DeGreiff, *Global Justice and Transnational Politics* (Cambridge, MA: The MIT Press).

Wertheimer, Alan (2008), 'Exploitation in Clinical Research', in Jennifer S.

Hawkins and Ezekiel J. Emanuel (eds), *Exploitation and Developing Countries* (Princeton, NJ: Princeton University Press).

Wolff, Jonathan (1998), 'Fairness, Respect, and the Egalitarian Ethos', *Philosophy and Public Affairs*, vol. 27, no. 2, pp. 97–122.

World Bank (1999), *World Development Report 1999/2000* (Oxford: Oxford University Press).

—(2003), *World Development Report 2003* (Oxford: Oxford University Press).

—(2011), *Level and Trends in Child Mortality*. Available at http://data.worldbank. org/indicator/SH.DYN.MORT, accessed 26 March 2012.

World Health Organization (2004), *The World Health Report 2004* (Geneva: WHO). Also available at http://www.who.int.whr/2004.

—(2007), *World Health Statistics* (Geneva: WHO). Available at http://www. who.int/gho/publications/world_health_statistics/whostat2007.pdf, accessed 26 March 2012.

INDEX

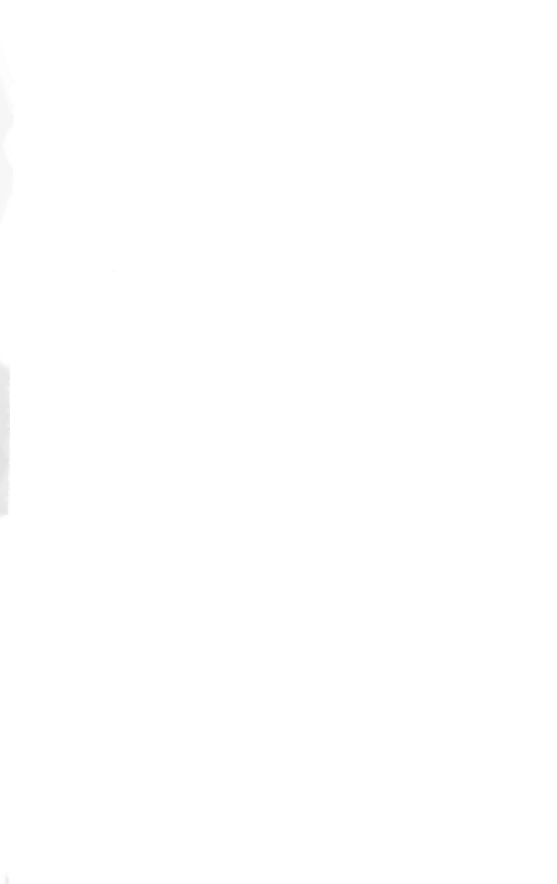